Men
at
Mid-Life

Men
at
Mid-Life
Steering
Through
the
Detours

James A. Harnish

DIMENSIONS
FOR LIVING

NASHVILLE

Men at Mid-Life:
Steering Through the Detours

Copyright © 1993 by Dimensions for Living

99 00 01 02 — 10 9 8 7 6 5

This book is printed on acid-free recycled paper.

Harnish, James A.
    Men at mid-life:steering through the detours/James A. Harnish.
    p.   cm.
    ISBN 0-687-06155-5 (alk. paper)
    1. Middle aged men—Religious life.   2. Midlife crisis—Religious aspects—Christianity.   3. Man-woman relationships—Religious aspects—Christianity.   4. Clergy—Psychology—Case studies.   5. Harnish, James A.   I. Title.   II. Title: Men at midlife.
BV4579.5.H37   1993
248.8'42—dc20   92-46043

Most scripture quotations are from the New Revised Standard Version Bible, Copyright 1989 by the Division of Christian Education of the National Council of the Churches of Christ in the USA. Used by permission.
    Those noted GNB are from the Good News Bible—Old Testament: Copyright © American Bible Society 1976; New Testament: Copyright © American Bible Society 1966, 1971, 1976.

MANUFACTURED IN THE UNITED STATES OF AMERICA

For brothers by birth—Jack, who has been with me from the beginning, and Terry, who has a few miles to go before mid-life . . . and brothers by grace—some named in this book and some named in my soul.

Then Joseph said to his brothers, "Come closer to me."
And they came closer. He said, "I am your brother."

Genesis 45:4

CONTENTS

ACKNOWLEDGMENTS

I am grateful for traveling companions who have strengthened my weak knees and straightened my path, including eight ruthlessly honest, laughter-addicted, faith-stretching soul-brothers who, like Chaucer's pilgrims on the way to Canterbury, tell their tales in a winter solstice retreat. To Dan Johnson, Bob Bushong, Tim Smiley, Gary Spencer, Wayne Curry, Rob Parsons, Jeff Stiggins, and John Hill: Thanks, and cheers!

Friends such as Chris Crotty, Phil Roughton, and Dick Wills keep me honest and whole. Leonard I. Sweet keeps me in touch with the postmodern world; Charles Killian keeps me laughing at it; and South African Bishop Peter Storey keeps my eyes focused on the kingdom of God coming within it.

A traveler's toast to the women who share my journey: my wife, Marsha, who told me to have my mid-life crisis and make the most of it, and who enters into the dialogue at the end of each of these chapters. Our daughters, Carrie Lynn and Deborah Jeanne, helped me to grow up while they did. The women who make me grateful that God does not call all ordained ministers from the men's locker room include Annette Pendergrass, Barbara Riddle, Terri Hill, and Charlene Kammerer. By being real women in ministry, they continually help me to be real as a man.

In the end, my "song of the open road" is a psalm of praise:

ACKNOWLEDGMENTS

I say to the LORD, "You are my Lord;
  I have no good apart from you." . . .
The boundary lines have fallen for me in pleasant places . . . .
You show me the path of life.
  In your presence there is fullness of joy;
  in your right hand are pleasures forevermore.

Psalm 16:2, 6, 11

James A. Harnish
Tampa, Florida

INTRODUCTION

If you are a man who is having a "mid-life crisis," or not yet experiencing a crisis but thinks he may be headed into one, this book is for you.

If you are a woman who wants to understand what on earth is going on with the man she loves and needs encouragement and help for "making it through the crisis," this book is for you.

If you are a man who wants to make the most of mid-life and needs resources from biblical faith to guide him through the transitions and changes of his life journey, this book is for you.

If you are a woman who wants to help the man in her life grow spiritually through the changes of mid-life, this book is for you.

If you are a couple who genuinely want to move toward deeper love for each other and stronger faith in God while steering through the detours of mid-life, this book is for you.

If you are still with me, then you have decided that this book is for you. But what does this book have to offer? Let me begin by telling you a little about its author.

I am one incredibly normal, moderately self-conscious, middle-aged, middle-class, Anglo-American male, with hair that is thinning and turning gray, who lives with awestruck wonder and gratitude for the staggering miracle of his own unrepeatable life.

This book is the travelogue of my own detour through

what is commonly called the male mid-life crisis, a detour I experienced while serving as pastor of a growing church in Orlando, Florida. I share my story not because it is unique, but because it is typical of men who, midway through their life journey, are forced to stop in the traffic to check the road map, examine the directional signs, smell the fumes of their past, and determine where in heaven's name they are going. It's a story of detours that take us to places we never intended to go, unexpected people we bump into along the way, and dangerous potholes that threaten to damage the transmission. Surviving, sometimes thriving on, the changes that come midway through our journey, we can take the wheel again with better understanding of what makes this machine go, and a new excitement for what lies ahead.

In addition to my own experience, this book grows out of professional and personal friendships with men on the mid-life journey—and the women making the journey with them—who have shared their stories, joys, and frustrations, and have allowed me to grow in faith with them.

But why write it down? What can I offer that hasn't already been said about the changing roles of women and men?

I identify with theologian Robert McAfee Brown, who said, "We write because we want to change things. We write because we have this arrogant but absolutely essential conviction that our curious little marks and squiggles, read by others, can make a difference. The 'difference' may be a new perception of beauty, a new insight into self-understanding, a new experience of joy, or a decision to join the revolution."

My attempt to "change things" involves making a *practical* difference in the lives of men and of their female traveling companions who are facing, or are in the midst of, a mid-life detour. Each chapter is followed by a conversation with my wife, Marsha, with whom I have shared this life journey for twenty-three years. These "He Said/She Said" conversations are nothing more nor less than our reflections on our experiences and the ideas expressed in each chapter, which we hope will model and encourage conversations for other couples. These conversations also set the stage for the "Action Plans for Him and Her," which suggest practical ways for men and women to integrate the content of each chapter into their own lives and relationships—both individually and together.

It is my hope that these "road signs" will help to make the journey more enjoyable and rewarding.

This travelogue of mid-life detours will not be worth the trees destroyed for its pages if it does nothing more than catalog the well-documented frustrations and fears, changes and challenges, of the mid-life experience. I also hope to "change things" by steering our conversations about maleness in the direction of the one absolutely exceptional model of mature manhood—the One who, at mid-life, journeyed into the desert wilderness of his own soul, faced death on a cross, and was awakened to new life on the third day.

My life-tested conviction is that the most powerful force in human experience is the self-giving, unconditional love of God made known in Jesus Christ. By fixing our sights on "the pioneer and perfecter of our faith," we may "lift [our] drooping hands and strengthen [our] weak knees, and make straight paths for [our] feet, so that what is lame may not be put out of joint, but rather be healed" (Heb. 12:2, 12-13).

There is no stopping place in this life . . . no, nor was there ever one for any man, no matter how far along his way he'd gone. This above all, then, be ready at all times for the gifts of God and always for new ones.

—Meister Eckhart

13

CHAPTER 1

Caution: Detour Ahead!

Psalm 102:6-7

I am like an owl of the wilderness,
like a little owl of the waste places.
I lie awake;
I am like a lonely bird on the housetop.

Did you see the Beatles on the "Ed Sullivan Show"?
Were you still in school when John Kennedy was shot?
Did you (or someone you knew) go to Woodstock?
Can you remember your draft lottery number?
Do you know the questions with answers that are "Blowin'
in the Wind"?

Your responses may mark you as a "baby boomer" who
remembers when John Kennedy said that the light had
been passed to a new generation. While we were still
young, JFK's light had been snuffed out, the precursor of
the shadow that would fall over the late sixties.

Anybody here seen my old friend Bobby?
Can you tell me where he's gone?

The years have passed. Mortgaged to our earlobes, with
a home in the suburbs, career promotions on the wall, and

kids in college, we who were supposed to have it all find ourselves crashing into a brick wall labeled "mid-life crisis."

Warning Signs

I had read the stories in every periodical, from *Good Housekeeping* to *Psychology Today*; I had watched the talk-show interviews in which every man sounded like the whining yuppies on "Thirtysomething." As a pastor, I had observed men in my own congregation making the same obvious and sometimes obnoxious mistakes as everyone else. I could read the signs. The calls of distress began to have a familiar ring.

A frustrated wife is shocked by the behavior of the man she married. She complains, "All these years, I thought I was doing what he wanted: taking care of the kids, cleaning the house, washing his clothes, standing beside him at those tedious business parties. I knew our marriage wasn't perfect, but he was never around when I really needed him. Now he says he hasn't been happy for years, that he needs to 'find himself,' and I was the only person who didn't know he was having an affair!"

An adult son or daughter couldn't believe what they saw their father doing: "Who does he think he is? Mom hangs in there with him all these years, and then, just about the time they could really start enjoying life, he quits his job, buys a sports car, and runs off with a single mother whose kids could be his grandchildren!"

Sometimes the call of distress comes from the man himself: "What's wrong with me? Everything is a pale shade of gray. I don't have any energy or drive. Nothing seems to matter. It's all coming apart around me, and I don't know what to do."

It seemed so obvious. I wondered why these guys couldn't see the flashing yellow lights and read the caution signs. Hadn't they noticed the wreckage other men had left along the curb? Didn't they have enough sense to steer clear of the potholes and keep their eyes on the road? When a friend handed me another article on male mid-life crisis and suggested I preach on it, I thanked him and promised to get around to it, but I was really thinking, "Don't count on it!"

Then I experienced it myself. With the notable exception of marital infidelity, I discovered that most of what they say about male mid-life crisis is true.

I cannot pinpoint the exact time or place the detour began. It was like C. S. Lewis's description, in *The Screwtape Letters*, of the road to Hell: "The safest road to Hell is the gradual one—the gentle slope, soft underfoot, without sudden turnings" (p. 56). There were warning signs along the way, to say nothing of the yellow flags my wife kept waving in front of me, but I was too busy being an overachiever to listen; too preoccupied with everything "out there" to be fully conscious of what was going on "in here"; too consumed by the excitement, the challenge, and the satisfaction of my work with others to be fully sensitive to my own needs. The clarity with which I could see what was happening in other men's lives became the illusion behind which I hid from my own. Even when I discovered I was headed down a side road, I thought I could steer back onto the highway with just a little more effort. All I had to do was try harder.

I felt like the cartoon character I discovered on the editorial page of the newspaper. Seated behind the steering wheel of his car while the highway patrolman was writing the ticket, he was saying, "It's a medical emergency, officer. I'm trying to get through a mid-life crisis!"

I kept smiling, kept denying the steely gray cloud closing in around me. I tried to find a quick spiritual fix through prayer and meditation. It would help, at least momentarily, but when my prayers were over, I would be back at it: driving, pushing, demanding more of myself than anyone else expected. I maintained a facade of the energy that had marked my life, but in the privacy of my office or home, I could feel the muscles of my face droop into a weary sag. When I sat down, I wanted to sit forever. I knew what the old gospel hymn writer meant when he sang, "How tedious and tasteless the hours." I began to feel like these psalmists:

> I am worn out, LORD . . . .
> I am as useless as a discarded wineskin.
>> Ps. 119:81, 83 GNB

> My life is disappearing like smoke . . . .
> I am beaten down like dry grass;
>> I have lost my desire for food. . . .
> I am like a wild bird in the desert,
>> like an owl in abandoned ruins.
> I lie awake;
>> I am like a lonely bird on a housetop.
>> Ps. 102:3-7 GNB

If I could rewind a videotape of the months before my crash, I would no doubt see what people around me saw: the gradual darkening beneath the eyes, the deepening stress-lines between the eyebrows, the shadowy paleness of the skin. A few courageous friends even cared enough to ask if I was all right.

But I was in denial. I energetically resisted the suggestion that I might not be at my best or at least in control of the situation. Who did they think was driving this car, anyway? There was no stopping me! I was a man on a mission, a noble knight with kingdoms to conquer, maidens to rescue, and windmills to tilt. So I kept driving until I drove right over the cliff.

The Crash

It was Sunday morning when the inevitable crash came. I awoke—or tried to—feeling like the coyote in the "Road-runner" cartoons, flattened by a steam roller and left like a pancake on the highway. Much of my existence during the next three weeks now seems a blur of high temperatures, coughing fits which left me exhausted and gasping, nausea brought on by my inability to tolerate the medications, and futile attempts to read the newspaper or watch TV. Not only did I not go to work; I didn't care. I could no longer silence my body's cry to do something to change my life-style and heal my soul.

The pop psychologists and TV comedians call it "male menopause." Dr. Martin Seligmann, writing in *Psychology Today*, called it Boomer Blues. In *Fortysomething*, Dr. Ross Goldstein describes it as "the descending curve of discontent." Weldon Gaddy said it was "a soul under siege." The labels are as diverse as the specific ways we experience it, but the common elements include a general sense of disillusionment with what has been, dissatisfaction with the way life is, a loss of energy or spirit, increased anxiety over aging and/or death, and often, as in my case, physical exhaustion and emotional depression.

My physician graciously waited until he had treated the pneumonia to tell me the truth. "This wasn't such a bad virus," he said. "You should have been able to beat it, but you have worn yourself down so badly that you had nothing left to fight it. We have the pneumonia under control; have you considered talking with a psychologist?"

The pavement ended. The bridge was out. There was

nowhere to turn. The superpastor who had recommended counseling to so many others had ended up on the detour himself. The hardest part was that I knew that the diagnosis was correct.

He Said/She Said

Jim: Well, what do you think? Did I describe my situation accurately?

Marsha: I don't remember seeing the physical effects as dramatically as you describe them, but I do remember your constantly talking about being tired and stressed by your work. You weren't much fun to live with; I wanted to laugh more. That's why I became more independent and was willing to go have a good time with other friends, particularly some who were more laid-back than you were. I needed it for my own well-being.

Do you think you were trying to keep up with the overachievers around you? Did you have a need to prove that you did your work as well as they did theirs?

Jim: Not consciously. I think most of this was inside me. I was being driven by my own need for approval and perhaps a desire for influence or some kind of power. There's no question that the environment in which we lived contributed to it, but most of it came from inside me.

What were some of the specific ways you tried to slow me down or turn me around?

Marsha: In the beginning, I became angry that you were gone so much. Then I decided that was only making me miserable, so I chose not to nag anymore. That doesn't mean that I didn't keep trying to remind you to lighten up, read some frivolous stuff which had nothing to do with theology or sermons, get out and play with your kids, take the boat out—basically, to enjoy living in Florida! I also decided that I would put up with only a certain amount of "work talk" when you came home in the evening. I wanted to be interested and supportive of your work, but I did not want it to be our only topic of conversation.

Jim: Thinking about our other male friends, would you say that this whole business of mid-life crisis is overplayed?

Marsha: It depends on the individual. For men who are overachievers, not at all. I get real tired of them. They take themselves too seriously. Laid-back people won't change the world, but they probably will live longer. You over-achievers may change the world, but you'll probably die young doing it. I think you are finally learning that lesson.

Action Plans for Him and Her

Him: Check things out. Take a good long look in the mirror and be honest about what you see. What does your face tell you about what might be going on inside your life? Share your concerns openly and honestly with God. If it's been more than a year since your last physical, schedule one with a physician who will be totally honest with you about your overall physical and emotional condition.

Him/Her: Ask and listen. Talk to your spouse or a trusted friend about what is going on in your life, and listen to what this person says. What signs of excessive stress has each of you noticed? Are you concerned about each other's overall well-being? Honest sharing is the first step toward understanding and healing.

Him/Her: Search the scriptures. To set your journey in the context of biblical thought and faith, begin reading through the psalms in a contemporary translation. Listen for the emotions; catch the feelings of the writers. When you find a psalm that describes the condition of your own soul (or that of your spouse/friend), settle in with it for a few minutes of personal reflection. Consider sharing your thoughts with your spouse or a friend.

Him/Her: Begin a journal. It doesn't need to be long or fancy; a simple notebook will do. Begin writing down reflections on your daily experiences and how you feel about them. Review your entries periodically to get a sense of how your life, attitudes, emotions, and perspectives are changing.

CHAPTER 2

Is Your Life-style Worth Dying For?

Luke 9:25

What does it profit them if they gain the whole world, but lose or forfeit themselves?

Jesus asked this probing question mid-way through his ministry, when he turned from his success in Galilee and headed toward Jerusalem and the cross.

The same question was asked by cardiologist Robert S. Eliot, director of Preventive and Rehabilitative Cardiology at St. Luke's Hospital in Phoenix. His book on the relationship between heart attack and stress simply asks: Is it worth dying for? "What does it profit them . . . ?"

American males in the 1990s die about seven years earlier than do women. Male incidence of suicide, chemical dependency, and violent death is grossly higher than that of women. When hospitalized, we stay 15 percent longer than women hospitalized for the same illness. Heart attack, generally the result of stress, smoking, and diet, continues to be the number-one killer of American men. James B. Nelson, in *The Intimate Connection*, concludes that "of the ten leading causes of death, it appears that only one [diabetes] is not significantly associated with the masculine role" (p. 13).

The Success Syndrome

After treating rich and successful people for more than a decade, Harvard psychologist Steven Berglas described individuals who suffer from "the success syndrome." By the world's standards, they reach the epitome of success, but they seem to carry the seeds of their own self-destruction. His examples read like the index of *People* magazine.

In *The Male Midlife Crisis: Fresh Start After Forty*, psychologist Nancy Mayer, out of her years of experience, reaches this disturbing conclusion:

> It is time to face the facts: In America today some of our most prized values are poisonous, and some of our most beloved legends are lies . . . the imperative of the work ethic twists men's lives into a combative, competitive struggle, leaving little time or energy for pleasurable pursuits. . . . The traditional male role, which says a man must be a super-achiever, striving incessantly for power and success, leads too often to the death of the man's spirit. Or to death itself. (pp. 66-67)

"What does it profit them . . . ?" It's no coincidence that Jesus raised this question midway through his career, following immediately on the heels of enormous success in Galilee. That's the time most of us face it, too.

Driving Forces Within

I've always been a high-energy, compulsive sort of guy. Looking back on my college days, I have to agree with one of my roommates who, years later, told me that I was so busy overachieving that no one could really get to know me. By divine providence, subconscious awareness of my need, or some mysterious combination of the two, I fell in love with and married a woman whose competence is not competitive and whose self-worth does not depend on the adrenalin of overachievement.

I was also drawn to male friends, fellow college and graduate students, who awakened the quieter, more reflective part of my personality. Although they could not reduce the driving forces within me, those relationships did give me a taste for a more contemplative life and an appreciation for a less frenetic pace, which continues to balance my achievement-oriented personality.

Halfway through my career, I have learned that institutions—including the church—thrive on the energy of compulsive workaholics. When I was appointed to the booming suburbs of Orlando in 1979, all that energy—some rooted in a healthy vision of Christian community and some emerging from unhealthy personal needs—was poured into beginning a new congregation. By the time we celebrated our tenth anniversary there, it was one of the most rapidly growing churches in Florida. The final accomplishment was the completion of a $5 million building program.

The consecration of the sanctuary was one of the great days of my life. We celebrated with an eighty-voice choir, a full orchestra, the herald trumpets from Walt Disney World, and two thousand people in the congregation. That church really knows how to throw a party!

The same friend who recommended that I preach on mid-life crisis told me that the accomplishment of that goal—the building program—should be enough to satisfy me for the rest of my career. It didn't require the skills of a psychotherapist to predict the onset of something like post-partum "blues" and the need for recovery time after such a demanding and emotional high, but there was no time for rest. I kept right on pushing until that Sunday morning when my body finally said, "No more!"

My physical condition forced upon me the question that had arisen many times before (most often from my wife!), but which I had only partially faced: What does it profit a man to gain the world but forfeit himself? What good is success, affirmation, influence, power, or anything else, if by gaining it we lose our physical health, our emotional balance, our spiritual wholeness, our closest relationships? What kind of bargain is it to gain temporary success but lose those things that are eternal, the things that are most essential to life?

I knew that I needed help. Rather than turn to the counselors to whom I had referred so many other people, I found my therapist the way others did—by reference from a pastor. When I walked into his office for the first appointment, he did not know my name or my profession. All that mattered was that I was a depressed person who needed help.

He listened patiently as I described the same condition he had heard from so many other men. Then he looked me in the eye and said, "Well, you have good reasons to be depressed. Let's go to work on them."

Gradual Transformation

My wife and I call 10:47 P.M. (eastern time) Personality Transformation Time for the TV dramas. That is the crisis moment when problems that have been dramatized in lurid detail for forty-five minutes are suddenly transformed in a climactic emotional confrontation. After a sixty-second commercial break, the characters return in marvelous wholeness and harmony.

I'm convinced that in the real world, 10:47 P.M. hardly

ever comes. Personalities are seldom transformed during a sixty-second commercial break. I wish I could describe one great turning point in those counseling sessions, one dramatic conversion moment when, like the conversion of Saul on the Damascus Road (Acts 9), I was blinded by the light of my own condition and transformed into a new person. I'm sure it happens that way for some people, although when you read the story more closely, you discover that it did not really happen that way for Paul. His Personality Transformation Time actually began when he witnessed the stoning of Stephen, and it continued through his developmental time with Ananias and the three years in the desert.

For most of us, the expectation of a dramatic "conversion" is destined for disappointment. Personal transformation usually comes gradually as we walk down well-beaten paths, discovering things we have been too busy to see. New life emerges slowly as we study the map of our lives and choose new roads to follow. New growth often takes shape in human personalities the same way it does in nature, like the mustard seed growing slowly into a flourishing bush.

A Central Attitude Shift

Looking back across this journey toward wholeness, I can see at work in my life the principle that Jesus describes in the first half of that mid-life quotation: "Those who want to save their life will lose it, and those who lose their life for my sake will save it" (Luke 9:24).

If we try to save life—hold it tightly, squeeze it, force it, push it, demand success on some arbitrary scale—we will destroy it, cramp it, squeeze the life right out. But if we learn to lose life—to set it free, release it, give it to something larger than our own self-interest—we will save it. We will experience that salvation which the Bible intends—salvation that results in wholeness of life and relationships.

One of the great saints of Christianity in the twentieth century, E. Stanley Jones was a global person who saw his faith and life in a universal context. When asked what is at the heart of life and the universe, he named self-giving love: He believed that the self-giving love of God in Jesus Christ "is not marginal, occasionally seen, but it is at the very 'heart' of final power. God is love and works by love, and by nothing else than love."

Jones told the story of a particularly difficult flight in miserable weather. Everyone except the stewardess, Jones, and his companion were sick. When the weather calmed, his companion began to sing to himself. A sick passenger behind him could stand it no longer, and blurted out, "No one has a right to be as happy as you are!" Jones' friend had replied that the sick passenger was correct. Speaking of his own life, Jones wrote in *Song of Ascents,* "In this Song of Ascents not one single note is here by right. I deserve nothing; I have everything. God is the heart of this everything. I have everything—everything I need, and more" (p. 23).

One of the central attitude shifts required to make possible the life which Jesus described is that one must begin to see all of life as a marvelous gift from the God who places self-giving love at the center of the universe. In receiving and sharing that love, we find life that can never be lost.

The chapters that follow track the journey I've been making through mid-life, toward the wholeness and salvation the Bible intends. Because my journey is not unique but is typical of so many men, I describe some of the road signs I defined in therapy and which I am attempting to follow in order to move from a life-style worth dying for to a life that is actually worth living.

He Said/She Said

Marsha: I understand your description of the overachieving personality (women can have this kind of personality, too). Do you think people who are less compulsive, more laid-back, can experience as much as, or more satisfaction and happiness than you do?

Jim: I think there is a good possibility that the more relaxed folks are happier. I don't think it's happiness that drives us. I think we are more driven by internal needs for accomplishment and are more oriented toward the satisfaction of seeing work completed. Do you ever experience the kind of compulsive drive I've described here?

Marsha: When I see you and some of your friends receive the recognition for your success, I have moments when I feel envious, but then I realize that I'm not willing to pay the price that all of you pay for your success. I figure life is too short to work that hard.

Jim: Spoken like a first-class second-born child! I think that's why I married you!

Marsha: Maybe that's why I married you, too. Perhaps we choose partners because they complement us. If I had married a more laid-back person, there is a possibility that I would end up being more driven, the way you are now. Sometimes when I am around more relaxed folks, I am frustrated by their casual approach to responsibility and want to get them moving. I have a real need to get things done, but I don't allow myself to be overloaded with responsibilities. That's the main difference. I don't take on more than I think I can handle.

Jim: What can a woman do to help a man who struggles with the "success syndrome," and still keep her sanity?

Marsha: I've learned to live with a certain amount of freedom from the need to control your compulsions, while still encouraging you to find ways to relax, get away from your work, and become interested in other things. I guess I've been pretty much a failure at the latter, but I keep trying!

Action Plans for Him and Her

Him/Her: Dr. Mark Trotter offers four things to remember when we face times of stress:

- Remember that what you are facing is not unique to you. . . . Most everybody faces problems in this life that they can't solve. . . . [People] who are spiritually mature, at one time faced what you are facing now.
- Remember that you are a human being, not a superman or a superwoman. . . . Justification by faith means that all that is expected of you is that you do your best, and leave the rest to God.
- Remember, though you are not in control, God is.
- Be patient. . . . Watch for something to happen that you never planned.

Him: Spend a few minutes asking yourself what you might be at risk of forfeiting for the sake of whatever you define as "success." Then focus your attention on Luke 9:24 and honestly describe what Jesus' words might mean for you. Record your thoughts. Repeat this exercise when you sense yourself becoming overwhelmed by the need to "succeed."

Him: Reflect on your internal needs for accomplishment and recognition. Think about how you might get things done without overloading yourself with responsibilities. This week, identify one task you can delegate to someone else, or find a creative way to accomplish your goals without over-committing yourself.

Her: If the man in your life is an overachiever, free yourself from the need to control his compulsions while encouraging him to find ways to relax, get away from his work, and devote time to relationships and recreational pursuits. Remember that all you can do is *encourage*. Regardless of *his* choices, nurture your own well-being by doing these things for yourself.

Him/Her: Limit the time you spend discussing work with the woman/man in your life. Although it is important to share this significant part of your life and to show interest and support for each other, work should not be the only topic or the dominant topic of conversation between you. Consider this: What would you talk about if your job were taken away?

CHAPTER 3

Driving Through the Desert

Luke 4:1-2a

Jesus, full of the Holy Spirit, returned from the Jordan and was led by the Spirit in the wilderness, where for forty days he was tempted by the devil.

The most emotion-packed literary journey I've taken was the desperate trek across the desert with the Joad family in John Steinbeck's masterpiece, *The Grapes of Wrath.* I could feel the heat, taste the sandy air, and experience the passionate, soul-shaking fear that kept them going.

While narrating their journey, Steinbeck traveled through the desert of his own soul. Entries like these appear throughout his journal, *Working Days*:

Feel pretty good but am impatient about all the things hanging over me. . . . I only hope that I am worthy to work . . . .

I feel like letting everything go. . . . My many weaknesses are beginning to show their heads. I simply must get this thing out of my system. I'm not a writer. I've been fooling myself and other people. . . . This success will ruin me. . . . It probably won't last. (p. 56)

Mid-way through the novel, however, Steinbeck recorded this amazing affirmation in his journal: "This is probably the high point of my life if only I knew it." His sojourn in the wilderness produced what many consider to be the greatest American novel. The difficult days of his desert journey became the high point of his life. Perhaps that's what Joseph Campbell meant:

> It is by going down into the abyss
> that we recover the treasures of life.

Wrestling in the Wilderness

Steinbeck's words describe what many of us feel during the mid-life transition. In spite of apparent success, we face raging insecurity, questioning whether we can keep going for the long haul. We become impatient with ourselves and with the people closest to us. We feel a weight hanging over us, most often the financial burden of the high cost of living. Weaknesses we have successfully denied begin to show their heads. There are times when we'd like to let everything go, but something in us keeps pushing on, like the Joads in their overloaded, overheated truck, with a psychological Ma Joad within, saying, "We gotta get across."

It's no coincidence to me that the Hebrews wandered for forty years in the wilderness, which means they arrived at the Promised Land when the offspring of the Exodus were at mid-life. Nor does it surprise me that the Spirit drove Jesus into the wilderness where he wrestled with the same issues we face at mid-life.

Within the dramatic imagery of Luke's account of Jesus' desert experience (4:1-13), we can feel the inner turmoil of a person who wrestles with the devils of temptation. Turning stones into bread to satisfy physical hunger raises the question of what is most important in our lives: satisfying our physical needs or the needs of our souls? The satanic promise of fawning attention from "all the kingdoms of the world" raises the issue of who or what we will worship, honor, and obey, and what price we will pay for pride and power. The tempting possibility of one great miracle that will prove God's authority uncovers our search for a short-cut to success that will avoid the tough demands of living.

Beneath it all is the tension between success and failure: How much of your integrity will you trade to get to the top? And the tension between means and ends: Does an honorable goal justify dishonorable methods? And the tension between the abuse of power and wise stewardship: Will you use the resources God provides for selfish purposes?

It is also no surprise to me that before the middle-aged Saul could claim his new identity as the apostle Paul, he spent three years in the desert, sorting through the reorientation of his life that followed his conversion.

These wilderness stories are not true because they are in the Bible; they are in the Bible because they are true to our human experience. The journey toward wholeness usually includes a time of wandering, searching, wrestling in the wilderness. In *Fortysomething*, Ross E. Goldstein writes that "if we think of midlife transition as a psychological journey, then it starts with getting lost" (p. 43).

The desert terrain forces questions of survival upon us. What will it take to get through? How can we discover the presence of One who can make of our time in the wilderness one of the best times of our lives?

Discovering Our Dependence

The desert is that place in our experience where we discover our dependence. We are forced to acknowledge that there are no "self-made" men. We abandon our illusions of absolute independence and face our human limitations, the

34

pain of personal failure, the loneliness that comes in knowing we are not ultimately as indispensable as we pretend to be. In the desert we discover our dependence on God and on other persons for wholeness and life. The Hebrew poet captured the feeling of this desert experience:

> My soul thirsts for God,
> for the living God. . . .
> My tears have been my food
> day and night,
> while people say to me continually,
> "Where is your God?"
> Psalm 42:2, 3

My physical collapse came at the most critical time of the church year: the annual stewardship crusade, an energetic month of activities, much of which had appeared to be dependent upon my personal leadership. Now I was flat on my back, barely able to answer the telephone. I was down for the count, and I didn't even care.

You can guess the rest of the story. With my absence, other persons came on board. Leadership abilities that had been hidden behind mine began to emerge. It would be dishonest to say that everything went off without a hitch, and it would be artificially humble to say that my presence was not missed, but the task was accomplished. More important, I realized again that I am made of flesh, that I am not indispensable, and that I am utterly dependent upon God and other people.

Discovering Our Vulnerability

The desert is also a place where we discover our vulnerability. Looking back through my journal entries in the year prior to my own "crash," I can see my growing free-

35

dom to reveal my own weakness, to share my exhaustion, to unmask my own need. As I reflected on Psalm 42 for one entry, I wrote:

> I know what the psalmist means, Lord. I am weary—bone weary, exhausted after all we have done. I'm acknowledging that, Lord—owning it, sharing it, and expressing gratitude for the understanding I receive. . . . I need this quiet space, this silence. Help me to place my trust, hope, and confidence in you, so that one day I will again praise you, my help and my God.

As I look back now, I cannot remember who it was or how it came; but the journal entry bears witness that when I acknowledged, owned, and shared my weariness, I received understanding.

Genuine vulnerability does not mean wallowing in self-centered pain or spilling the bile of our frustrations on everyone we meet. It does not mean making a virtue of our weakness in a way that manipulates others' compassion for our own ends. It simply means having the honesty to acknowledge our feelings and express them to someone else. Steinbeck described it in the privacy of his journal, but he also shared it in the intimacy of his closest relationships. In the same way, the psalmist shares his feelings with God and, through his poetry, with all of us. There is a ruthless honesty about these words:

> My soul is cast down within me . . . .
> Deep calls to deep
>   at the thunder of your cataracts;
> all your waves and your billows
>   have gone over me. . . .
> I say to God, my rock,
>   "Why have you forgotten me?"
>   Psalm 42:6a, 7, 9

I am convinced that the most common male roadblock on the way to wholeness is a barricade marked, "Don't stop now, you are invulnerable!" Sometimes it takes a journey through the desert to break down our defenses, to strip away our masks, and to finally enable us to acknowledge for ourselves and with others the deep hurts and hungers of our souls.

Discovering Gratitude

It's clear enough that the way through the wilderness might teach us dependance and vulnerability. But the thought of finding gratitude in the desert may take us by surprise. Gratitude in hunger and thirst? Appreciation through loneliness? Thanks on the desert journey?

The answer, of course, is **Yes**! Genuine gratitude is born from a deep appreciation of the infinite value of what is left after everything trivial, everything artificial, everything inconsequential has been stripped away. Gratitude is the emotion that floods our souls when we see what we have in the light of what we have—or could have—lost.

We need not make the religious pilgrimage to the Temple in Jerusalem to feel the passion of the psalmist as he remembers:

> How I went with the throng,
>   and led them in procession to the house of God,
>   with glad shouts and songs of thanksgiving.
>   Psalm 42:4

The memory of it, now that he is in exile, multiplies its value for him.

I worked on the final draft of this manuscript as Hurricane Andrew was bearing down on the south Florida coast, bringing with it the worst devastation in this century. In the aftermath of the storm, I talked with pastors and friends whose neighborhoods, businesses, and homes were wiped off the map. Although nothing can replace what has been lost, each of them expressed some way in which their incalculable loss has increased their sense of gratitude for the things that are left. They will emerge from the wreckage with a new sense of appreciation for what they have, in the shadow of what they have lost.

Thumbing through the library in search of something else, I discovered, as if by accident, a poem by W. H. Auden, which nurtures the desert places in my own soul. It was composed in response to the death of his literary hero, William Butler Yeats.

In describing his own journey through the wilderness, Auden invites us to go with him "to the bottom of the night." We feel what he calls "a rapture of distress." But in his closing lines, he discovers a source of healing in the wilderness:

> In the deserts of the heart
> Let the healing fountain start . . . .

His darkness turns toward the light; his sorrow is transformed into praise . . . the healing fountain of praise.

Thomas Merton once said, "Alas, in America there is no wilderness, only dude ranches." This was his description of the way we will do almost anything to avoid the wilderness, to anesthetize the pain of reality, to find a detour around the desert. Commenting on Merton's words, William Sloan Coffin remarked:

What Merton was getting at was this: Americans are afraid of being alone for fear of having to pay a call on themselves and finding no one at home! But imagine finding at home not only yourself, but God and Jesus, too. Wouldn't that take care of just about everything, from a clear direction for your life to the best possible company along the way?

Yet the healing fountain of praise springs up in the desert, the place where we discover our dependence, acknowledge our vulnerability, and learn to live with gratitude.

He Said/She Said

Jim: What about women? Do they go through the desert, too? Or are they always like Ma Joad, the one who holds things together and gives strength to everyone else?
Marsha: I think women need to journey through the desert, too. The problem is that sometimes their circumstances or the people around them won't allow them to get out of the nurturing, caretaking role. I think what you describe is necessary for anyone who wants to grow and become a mature person.
Jim: How is the journey different for women?
Marsha: The biggest difference is that women tend to be more vulnerable in their relationships with other women than men are with other men. As soon as I begin to feel "down," I share that with one of my friends. You men have a harder time opening up and expressing your needs with one another, so things tend to build up inside you until it becomes a major problem, or you ignore it all together. The point being that the "desert" experience may not be as dramatic for women as you describe here.

Action Plans for Him and Her

Him/Her: If you have not begun a spiritual journal, try it today. Slowly and quietly, read Psalm 42 in a contemporary translation. See if you can empathize with the psalmist's feelings. When you find a place where you do, describe how you feel. Then address your own prayer to God.

Him/Her: Study the story of Jesus' wilderness journey in Luke 4:1-13. Can you hear his temptations in a way that makes them consistent with the conflicts you (your spouse/friend) face? How does Jesus' response to his temptations help you in facing yours (in dealing with those of your spouse/friend)?

Her: Reflect on these questions and, if you choose, discuss your thoughts with the man in your life:

- Has his "desert experience" forced you into the desert as well? How would you describe this desert? What will you require to "make it through" this desert?
- Do you see yourself in the role of nurturer/caretaker? How does this role affect your relationship with the man in your life during his desert journey? Do you feel the need to "take care" of him, to "get him through" the desert? How do you feel about this? What would you like your role to be?

CHAPTER 4

Is Your Dad Still Behind the Wheel?

I John 2:9-10 GNB

Whoever says that he is in the light, yet hates his
[father], is in the darkness to this very hour.
Whoever loves his [father] lives in the light.

When I was preparing for that adolescent rite of passage called "getting your license"—which is, for a sixteen-year-old, the justification for existence—my dad tried to teach me to drive. We went to an uncompleted section of what one day would be Interstate 80. It could have been Armageddon! I'm not sure whether the conflict was due to my father's inadequacy as a teacher or my unwillingness to learn, but it didn't take long for us to decide that I needed to develop my driving skills in Mr. Murphy's Driver's Ed. class.

The memory comes back to haunt me whenever I feel the urge to remind my daughter of the speed limit or ask if she plans to put her foot on the brake before reaching the intersection. Following their father's example, both my daughters took Driver's Ed. at their high school!

The conflict over who is behind the wheel is a practical paradigm for the father/son conflict which is often at the core of the mid-life struggle. The most painful part of our journey toward wholeness may involve facing our fathers and deciding who is really behind the wheel.

Arthur Miller's *Death of a Salesman* revolves around the gut-wrenching struggle between Willy Loman and his oldest son, Biff. In the climactic confrontation, Biff pulls away and runs up the stairs in tears. Willy just sits there—passionless, emotionally distant, shrugging his shoulders and looking to his wife, Linda.

After a long pause, Willy stammers, "Isn't that—isn't that remarkable? Biff—he likes me!"

Linda interprets: "He loves you, Willy!"

And Happy, the younger brother, completes the thought: "Always did, Pop."

When Brendan Gill reviewed the Broadway production for *The New Yorker* several years ago, he commented that the actors' lines were almost lost because of the sound of people sobbing around him. That emotional response indicates that Arthur Miller's play touches a raw nerve in the American male psyche, penetrating the dark void which many men experience in their relationship with their fathers.

It's not as if our fathers were bad or abusive men. Most were the product of their times. Their understanding of manhood was forged on the anvil of the Great Depression. They were driven by the desire to produce, to provide, to ensure a better life for their children. They were honest, rule-keeping, God-fearing, patriotic folks who knew what was expected and did their job very well! But they often did so at the price of emotional intimacy.

My dad was the son of a coal miner. Knowing that college was beyond his financial reach, he went to work behind the counter of Mr. Bowman's auto-parts store, intending, I suppose, to continue his education later. For now, there was work to do, a living to earn, and, all too soon, a war to be won.

He married a young schoolteacher shortly after enlist-
ing, and the Army Air Corps shipped them to Florida.
They loved it. As a child, I was fascinated by a ragged old
album with its fading black-and-white photographs of a
slender young soldier and a young woman with a spectac-
ular smile and plunging neckline, leaning against a palm
tree hanging over the water at Silver Springs or standing
on the porch of a white frame house in Orlando. I had difficulty reconciling the romantic spirit of the pictures with
the intensely serious businessman who was always late for
supper and the hard-working housewife who would
finally tell us children to go ahead and eat without him.

They thought about living in Orlando after the war, but
instead, returned to the western Pennsylvania town in
which Dad had been born and would finally die. I felt a
mystical sort of completion to their story when, in the final
year of his life, they came to visit our new home in
Orlando. We walked around Lake Eola with his grand-
daughters, just as he had walked around it with his bride,
as if the road had come full circle and his journey had been
completed.

But there was no time for Sunshine State fantasies after
the war. Dad's younger brother—the good-looking
charmer with the day-brightening smile—had been shot
down in a B-52 over Holland. Their mother died a few
days later, probably from a broken heart. The old hometown was filled with returning GI's looking for work.
When Mr. Bowman offered Dad the old job, he took it.

Somewhere along the way, he considered preparing for
the ministry, a fact that forced me to wrestle with how
much of my calling came from my human father and how
much from the heavenly One. And he talked about having
twins. No one knows where he got that idea. But from
Orlando to Shanghai and back again, he had talked about
starting his family with twin boys. When it happened,

even he was so surprised that he left the receiver dangling from the old crank telephone in my grandfather's house to run to the hospital to make sure it was true.

His career path was set when he left Mr. Bowman and, with two other GI's as partners, formed a new business. For the rest of his life he poured his energy into the company store.

Sometimes we hated it. Family vacations were delayed because he had to make one more call. Sunday afternoon picnics were postponed for a mechanic who knew Ves would stop by the store after church and get a part for him. Coming home at night, we would stop to check the doors. Invariably, he'd find something which proved that if he didn't personally check on everything, it could all be lost.

I never doubted his love. It was as strong as his patriotism, his faith, and his teetotaling conviction against alcohol. I felt his inordinate pride, his strength of character, his rock-solid support. What I missed was his companionship. I have no memory of ever being alone with my father during those years. My mother was in charge; he was on the sidelines, the man in the shadows, "the wind beneath my wings." He loved his boys, but never changed their diapers. He was a prisoner of the Protestant work ethic, a compulsive workaholic whose identity and self-worth were inextricably bound to Clarion Automotive Supply Company.

Because my mother was such a dominant presence in my life, I grew up thinking that I was most like her; but as I worked my way through therapy, I realized how much I am my father's son. I work for a different company, but the compulsions are the same. I know the frustration of a wife who has had to hold supper because I squeezed in one more call, the daughters who wondered if I would be there in time to take them to gymnastics, the night I arrived at the swim meet just in time to see my eldest drying off from the best 500 meters of her high-school career. I changed my share of diapers, but when I compare myself to some of the younger fathers in my church, I know that I was just scratching the surface of "participatory fatherhood." Just about the time I think I've licked the addiction I inherited from my father, I find myself confessing it again.

Although I have long ago forgotten the source, a few lines of poetry have stuck in my memory from school days:

> As I was going up the stair,
> I saw a man who wasn't there.
> He wasn't there again today.
> I wish that man would go away.

Many of us discover that our fathers are the "man who wasn't there." Their ghosts still ride in the car. Sometimes we wrestle with their hands on the wheel as they continue to determine the direction of our journey. Sometimes they are the ghosts of remembered pain; sometimes the ghosts of forgotten losses; sometimes the ghosts of unfulfilled dreams. The sins of the fathers are visited on the second and third generations, not because God makes individual choices to punish our children with our mistakes, but because that's just how life is. We carry the scars our parents left. Part of the agenda for our mid-life journey is to settle the issue of whose hands are on the steering wheel of our lives.

Sam Keen describes his own encounter with his father through psychotherapy in his best-seller, *Fire in the Belly:*

The figures who inhabited my dreams became more real to me than those with whom I spent my daylight hours. My father, long dead, came to life again and we did battle. I found the courage to be angry with him for the wounds he had inflicted on me, to defy him, to break taboos, and finally to crawl so far inside the secret pain of his being that I could forgive and heal him by daring to do what he could not. (pp. 128-29)

While writing this chapter, I had lunch with a friend at a sidewalk cafe on the beach. As the ocean breeze blew across the table and the springtime sun warmed the air, he told me about a recent adult group that had wrestled with the Commandment to honor your mother and father. With the others in the group, he faced the pain in his relationship with his father. They concluded that the Commandment means we must honor the significance which those relationships have for us. Some are significant because they provide health, strength, and joy; others, because they contain incredible pain. Honoring may mean binding them into our lives, or it may mean wresting life from their control, but none of us can be whole persons until we "honor" those parental influences.

I honor my father with gratitude. I had my years of battle with him—some of it open between us, most of it inside myself. Through it all, Dad never changed. There were no surprises; he was utterly predictable. Beneath the things that could infuriate me were his undying pride for me, his love for my wife, and his joy in my children. God's work in my life across the months before Dad's death permitted me the grace to love him for who he was and the freedom to be the person I am called to be. I was given the all-too-rare gift of peace with my father, the freedom to say good-bye with nothing left undone between us.

A rugged Old Testament prophet named Ezekiel was fed up with one of the common assumptions of his time: "The parents have eaten sour grapes, and the children's teeth are set on edge." It's true enough; we can see it in our ordinary human patterns of existence. But Ezekiel believed that it did not need to be that way: "As I live, says the Lord God, this proverb shall no more be used by you. . . . Know that all lives are mine; the life of the parent as well as the life of the child is mine" (Ezek. 18:2, 3-4).

The words cut across the grain of the fatalistic assumptions of parent/child relationships and liberate us for the wholeness that comes by taking responsibility for our own lives. By God's grace, the only hands on the steering wheel can be your own.

He Said/She Said

Marsha: When I read this chapter, I almost cried because your description of your dad brought back so many memories of him. He was so proud of his sons, his daughters-in-law, and his grandchildren! I always felt his unconditional love and acceptance. I think that's what I miss most about him.

Jim: Yes, he did love the daughters we brought into his life! I sometimes think he was freer with his grandchildren than he was with his sons, but that is not unusual.

Marsha: I've heard you say that many men feel they are never able to live up to their father's expectations. Did you have to deal with that?

Jim: Not really, but then I went into the ministry, which met his expectations. I think the test came when we moved away rather than going back "home" after seminary. He accepted that pretty well.

Marsha: Yes, but remember the struggle your brother had when he went back "home" for a couple of years. The geographic distance may have made your situation easier.

Jim: Yes, and the fact that there are some things about me that he never knew!

Action Plans for Him

How do we face our fathers? Persons who have been sexually, physically, or emotionally abused need a competent psychotherapist. Assuming, however, that our fathers were good people whose understanding of fatherhood was shaped by their own experience, how can we begin to take the steering wheel into our own hands? These seven steps are a good beginning. Steps 1, 3, 5, and 6 may be shared with your spouse or a close friend. (Although I use the word *father*, these steps are also appropriate in facing a *father figure*.)

Step 1: Accept your father as an imperfect, fragile human being. Write about your recollections of him and your relationship with him. James B. Nelson, in *The Intimate Connection*, writes that "healing might come from consciously entering into our fathers' histories, finding out what life was really like for them and empathizing with their pain" (p. 44). A part of my own healing is reflected in telling Dad's story. By walking with him along the road he traveled, I have been set free to understand his experience and to value both his strengths and his weaknesses.

Step 2: Forgive and receive forgiveness. If not in person, in some deep corner of your psyche, allow the Spirit of the One who said, "Father, forgive them; for they do not know what they are doing," to enable you to say the same about your father. Genuinely forgive the things he has done and the things he has left undone—things it is now too late to change. After facing your own inadequacies as a son, accept your father's forgiveness and the forgiveness of God.

Step 3: Take inventory of the ways your father's attitudes and actions have been duplicated in you. You probably function out of many of the same attitudes and convictions. List these attitudes and convictions; claim those that are healthy and helpful and break away from those that are hurtful and destructive.

Step 4: Take action. Do something to express the healing you seek:

- Write a letter to your father expressing your feelings about your relationship. Make the letter very specific as you share both your gratitude and frustration. If he is still living, you can decide whether to mail the letter.
- Visit your father's hometown. Walk the streets he walked. Visit with people who are/were his friends and listen to their stories. Try to feel the tempo of the world in which he lived.
- If your father is deceased, visit his grave and "talk" to him about your life and your relationship with him.
- Spend an evening with the family picture album. Look for the expressions on your father's face. Try to put yourself in his place.
- If you have siblings, talk with them and compare notes on the similarities and differences in your feelings about your father, or do this with a trusted friend.

Step 5: Many of our assumptions of male roles in the family are reflections of the effects of sin that Adam and Eve experienced *outside* the garden (Gen. 3:14-19). The good news of the gospel is that new life is possible. We do not need to remain prisoners of our parental past. Instead of projecting our sin-damaged experiences of fatherhood onto God, we can begin with the Gospel and shape our fathering after the model revealed in Jesus' relationship with the God he called Father. Make clear choices to father your children in new, intentionally chosen, Christlike ways.

- Establish a discipline of prayer for your children and for God's help in parenting.
- Clear time on your calendar for an outing with your children. Take them to lunch, visit their schools or work-places, go to a football game or movie together, and so forth.
- If your children are young, take a parenting course. Get involved with other Christian parents in a study/fellow-ship group.
- Develop good listening skills so that you can hear what your children are saying.

Step 6: Read or watch a videotape of *Death of a Salesman, Long Day's Journey into Night,* or *Field of Dreams.* Can you identify with any of the characters? Share your own family story with your spouse or a close friend. Describe the factors that made your father the person he was. Attempt to feel his sense of failure or success. Allow yourself the privilege of expressed anger. Find the places where you can allow the grace of God to bring forgiveness, compassion, and healing for your relationship with your parents.

Step 7: Search for a place in your relationship with your father where you can apply this biblical affirmation:

> If we say that we have no sin, we deceive ourselves, and there is no truth in us. But if we confess our sins to God, he will keep his promise and do what is right: he will forgive us our sins and purify us from all our wrongdoing. . . . Whoever says that he is in the light, yet hates his [father], is in the darkness to this very hour. Whoever loves his [father] lives in the light, and so there is nothing in him that will cause someone else to sin. . . . I write to you, my children, because your sins are forgiven for the sake of Christ. I write to you, fathers, because you know him who has

existed from the beginning. I write to you, young men, because you have defeated the Evil One.

I John 1:8-9; 2:9-10, 12-13 GNB

Ask yourself these questions as you reflect on this passage from I John:

- What is the truth in my relationship with my father?
- What is my part in the "sin" in our relationship?
- What would it mean for me to "confess my sin to God" and thereby experience God's forgiveness?
- John compares loving to being in the light, and not loving to being in the darkness. Where am I on that continuum of light to darkness?
- What will it take for me to realize forgiveness in my relationship with my father or father figure?

Which Road Will You Choose?

Luke 9:51

*When the days drew near for him to be taken up,
he set his face to go to Jerusalem.*

"The Road Not Taken," by Robert Frost, is one of my favorite poems. You've probably read it, even if it was years ago in a junior-high English class.

> Two roads diverged in a yellow wood,
> And sorry I could not travel both
> And be one traveler, long I stood
> And looked down one as far as I could
> To where it bent in the undergrowth;
>
> Then took the other, as just as fair,
> And having perhaps the better claim,
> Because it was grassy and wanted wear;
> Though as for that, the passing there
> Had worn them really about the same,
>
> And both that morning equally lay
> In leaves no step had trodden black.
> Oh, I kept the first for another day!

Yet knowing how way leads on to way,
I doubted if I should ever come back.

I shall be telling this with a sigh
Somewhere ages and ages hence:
Two roads diverged in a wood, and I—
I took the road less traveled by,
And that has made all the difference.

They come to all of us, you know, those times of decision, those points of departure, those irrevocable
choices, those times when we—because we cannot travel
both roads—choose a particular path, and that choice
makes all the difference. We sense the truth of it during
mid-life because we begin to feel that the choices are
narrowing, the options are not as broad, the alternatives
fewer than they were before. When the roads diverge,
we make choices that can, as time goes by, make a great
difference.

Many of us tend to describe these kinds of choices
with forceful language, dramatic stories, soul-stirring
images; but not Frost. There is an uncomplicated stillness
about this poem, the quiet strength of one who looks
down the road and makes a choice that comes from
something deep inside which never can be fully deci-
phered or explained.

Although often our language may be dramatic, we too
know this quiet strength. If we are asked how we made a
decision, the odds are good that we will say, "I just felt I
had to do it. There was really no other way." I take that
response to mean that somewhere in the silence of our own
souls, we know that if we are to be consistent with the
deepest truth of our being, the truest stuff of our personality, the strongest roots of our convictions and values, then

it is hardly a choice at all. Behind, before, and beneath all the enticing alternatives is a quiet, solid, unwavering sense that this is the path we must take, the road we must follow. And that makes all the difference.

Knowing Which Path to Take

I feel the same sort of quiet decisiveness when I read Luke's description of Jesus' journey to Jerusalem. The gospel swings on the hinge of that decisive moment when Jesus "set his face to go to Jerusalem" (9:51). It's a strong, virile image of a person who knows that there is no other choice: This is the road he or she must take. And that makes all the difference. Until this point, the people have—by and large—been pleased with Jesus' performance; they like what they've seen and heard. He's been a success. But things begin to change now.

Jesus' advance team goes into a Samaritan village to prepare the way, just the way an advance team goes to town to prepare the way for the visit of a campaigning politician. Everything is fine until the villagers see Jesus coming down the road. They start to cheer, but when they look into his eyes their mood changes. Luke records: "They did not receive him, because his face was set toward Jerusalem" (9:53).

There's a fascinating follow-up scene in chapter 13. Some Pharisees—the folks who, according to Luke, want to do away with Jesus—come to him and say, "Get away from here, for Herod wants to kill you" (13:31).

My guess is that these Pharisees were decent, law-abiding folks who wanted to keep things in order. They may have been the kind who really don't care what people believe, think, or choose, as long as they don't disrupt the existing order, don't unhinge the traditions, don't cause any trouble. Maybe they were motivated by genuine concern. They didn't like Jesus, but they didn't want him to suffer, either. For whatever reason, they told Jesus to skip town, go in some other direction. "Don't go to Jerusalem!" they said.

There is no confusion about Jesus' response: "Go and tell that fox for me, 'Listen, I am casting out demons and performing cures today and tomorrow, and on the third day I finish my work. Yet today, tomorrow, and the next day I must be on my way, because it is impossible for a prophet to be killed outside of Jerusalem'" (13:32-33).

Jesus knows where he's going. He knows what lies ahead. There is no shifting of his course. He will go right on being who he is and doing what he is called to do, all the way to Jerusalem—all the way to the cross.

What does this story have to do with the choices we make during the mid-life journey? What keeps us going when the choices are difficult and the options few? What inspires our highest ideals? What motivates the strongest convictions of our lives? What is it that keeps us on the road less traveled when the going gets rough?

Finding a Place to Stand

I am convinced that it makes all the difference in the world if, behind all the options and beneath all the choices before us, there is one central choice around which all the other choices are ordered, one great motivating force that energizes the rest of the forces of human existence. The directional choices at mid-life are less traumatic, less likely to wreck our lives and shatter our relationships, if we have found "a place to stand," a solid center in the core of our being.

We get an insight into the soul of Jesus in the red-

55

blooded compassion of his words as he looks out over the Holy City: "Jerusalem! Jerusalem! . . . How many times I wanted to put my arms around all your people, just as a hen gathers her chicks under her wings, but you would not let me!" (13:34-35 GNB)

If we knew the Old Testament prophets as well as Jesus and Luke did, we could hear behind Jesus' words the voice of Hosea, who heard God say:

> When Israel was a child, I loved him
>   and called him out of Egypt as my son.
> But the more I called to him,
>   the more he turned away from me. . . .
> Yet I was the one who taught [them] to walk.
> I took my people up in my arms,
>   but they did not acknowledge that I took care of them.
> I drew them to me with affection and love.
>   I picked them up and held them to my cheek;
>   I bent down to them and fed them. . . .
> How can I give you up, Israel? . . .
>   My love for you is too strong.
>
> 11:1-4, 8a, c, GNB

That light in Jesus' face, that determined look in his eyes, that decisive energy in his step, that calm decisiveness in his soul—these were nothing more nor less than the tenacious love of God for his wandering, rebellious children—the love that will not let go. Everything else in Jesus' life was ordered around and motivated by the centrifugal force of that love.

That's why there was no other way for Jesus. That's why he set his face for Jerusalem. That's the silent necessity beneath his journey toward the cross. To be consistent with the love of God for this broken world, there was no other way. And when it comes down to it, that's hard to beat.

I know people who are driven by other things: pride, power, prestige, wealth. I know other convictions or emotions that can energize a person for action: fear, jealousy, patriotism, ambition. I know how unexpected circumstances can force a decision we may not be ready to make: job loss, physical illness, divorce, the death of someone we love. I know how the pressures of the mid-life experience can close in around us. But when it comes down to it, I can think of no more powerful, decisive, or hopeful force in human life than the self-giving, cross-bearing, life-empowering love of God revealed in Jesus Christ.

Following Jesus Along the Path

One of my personal heroes is Dag Hammarskjold, the visionary leader of the United Nations who died in a mysterious airplane crash while he was trying to negotiate a cease-fire between hostile forces in northern Rhodesia in 1961. His personal reflections are recorded in his *Markings*. Here's how he described the central decision in his life:

I don't know Who—or what—put the question, I don't know when it was put. I don't even remember answering. But at some moment I did answer YES to Someone—or Something—and from that hour I was certain that existence is meaningful and that, therefore, my life, in self-surrender, had a goal. From that moment I have known what it means "not to look back." . . . As I continued along the Way, I learned, step by step, word by word, that behind every saying in the Gospels stands one man and one man's experience. Also behind the prayer that the cup might pass from him and his promise to drink it. Also behind each of the words the Cross. (p. 205)

I am grateful that behind and beneath my own mid-life transitions there has been the solid center, the place to stand that is best described in an old gospel song: "I have decided to follow Jesus, No turning back! No turning back!" The deepest conviction of my life—born within me from my parents' faith, encouraged through a multitude of kid-loving adults during my adolescence, and forged on the anvil of my adult experience—is that if anyone ever got it right, if anyone ever lived the way God intended for human beings to live, if anyone ever held the key to eternal life, if ever there was anyone worth following on the journey of life, it was Jesus.

When the time came to choose; when I stood where two roads diverge and I knew I could not travel both; when it seemed that there was simply nowhere else to go, I am grateful for that "still point in the turning world," a point that is centered in my identity as a disciple of Jesus Christ. In this continually changing, steadily growing, and sometimes mysterious companionship, I have found a decisive path to follow. Through the depression, struggle, and transformation of my mid-life journey, I must bear witness to the central thought of his words, his way, his love, and his cross.

> I shall be telling this with a sigh
> Somewhere ages and ages hence:
> Two roads diverged in a wood, and I—
> I took the road less traveled by,
> And that has made all the difference.

He Said/She Said

Jim: Do you ever have the feeling that the choices are narrowing, that the choices are fewer than they once were?

Marsha: Yes. I think it is linked to having kids in college and realizing the multitude of options before them, apparently more options than we had or thought we had.

Jim: So, how do we deal with that?

Marsha: I like to think that I've made the right choices in my life and have been fine-tuning them throughout the years. That's not to say that you can't make changes at mid-life, but it's just harder to do. I know people who make those kinds of changes, and I admire them. It takes a lot of energy. Sometimes I think it would be neat to try something new, but I feel good about where I am. This points to why it is so important to prepare our children to make the wisest choices when they have the opportunity to make them.

Jim: I agree, but let's face it: They really don't ask for our help much anymore!

Marsha: They don't call and ask, "What should I do?" But all the work we've done across the years is influencing their choices. I hope we have helped build the framework on which they make those decisions. It doesn't mean we are going to stop praying that God will use the experiences we've shared in the past to help them choose their future.

I think it is important to acknowledge that unexpected circumstances, things over which we have little or no control, can cause us to face major life-changing decisions—things like divorce, death, job loss. We've been through this kind of thing with some very close friends recently. They didn't choose the circumstances they faced, but their faith is sustaining them, keeping them going, and helping them find a new and hopeful future. It's not easy, but they are making it, and sometimes that's what makes the difference.

The danger is that this chapter sounds kind of neat and tidy, as if you can see down the road and know what is ahead. It's one thing to look back and know where you've been, but sometimes things get pretty foggy and you can't really see what's out there ahead.

Jim: That's absolutely right. In fact, the folks I worry about are the ones who think they have it all perfectly clear ahead of time. My experience is that very seldom have we been absolutely sure of making the right choice. Most of the time, we've had to just start walking and keep our souls open for the ways God confirms that we are on the right path.

Action Plans for Him and Her

Him: What decisions must you make at this time in your life? List them on a piece of paper. Then put a mark beside those choices that must be made now and cannot be delayed. Beside each decision, describe the irrevocable consequences of this choice. Because many of these decisions will affect or involve your family, you may want to do this with your spouse or another family member.

Him: Is there a central commitment, a motivating force that orders and energizes your life? Write a description or definition of this central commitment. At the end of the week, list the practical effects this commitment has had on your actions.

Him/Her: Spend some time walking with Jesus through chapter 9 of Luke. As you identify with the disciples or with Jesus at any point of that story, record your thoughts on paper. Repeat this exercise periodically, as new experiences and choices enter your life.

Her: List the major choices that have shaped who you are now (e.g., marriage, divorce, career, children, education). Beside each choice, record some of the major influences that affected your decision. Who were the significant persons involved? How did they affect your choices?

Her: Reflecting on your present circumstances, how do you feel about yourself? What central commitments determine your response to your circumstances? Are there changes you need to consider in relationship to the man in your life?

CHAPTER 6

Whose Face Is on Your Driver's License?

Ephesians 2:4-5

But God, who is rich in mercy, out of the great love with which he loved us even when we were dead through our trespasses, made us alive together with Christ.

I could hardly believe it! I didn't think it could happen, but there it was, right in my hand. I looked at it again as I drove out of the parking lot. For the first time in my life, I had a driver's license with a picture of myself that did not look like a reject from the "Wanted" posters on the wall of the post office. This one actually looked like the person I think I am!

We all know the feeling. Whose face is that? What kind of person do I think I am? What defines my identity? Who tells me who I am?

External Expectations

The images of "the perfect male" bombard us every day. We are supposed to have some combination of Tom Crews' smile, Robert Redford's charm, Kevin Kostner's talent, and Daniel Day-Lewis's *Last of the Mohicans* chest. The permanently skinny seventh-grader within me didn't find much encouragement when *The New York Times* magazine presented the leading fashions for the 1990s man, most of which include macho-styled shirtless vests and buttonless shirts that are supposed to "celebrate his core of individuality." The fashion authorities instructed that the clothing makes physical fitness mandatory.

Although almost no one I know could ever live up to the images of the perfectly honed models, their very pictures on the magazine pages reflect a society in which appearances are everything, where the "look" is what counts—a society where men (and women) measure themselves on a standard of perfection that would leave Adonis running for cover.

And running is what most of us do. But poet Robert Bly believes that "the American man wants to stop running; he wants a few moments of peace. . . . He has a tremendous longing to get down to his own depths." We wear ourselves out attempting to live up to some external model of manhood, while at the same time longing to discover the silent space within that will define who we really are.

Most of us grew up watching movies that starred John Wayne—the archetype of the strong, stoic cowboy. Then along came Alan Alda— the caring, sensitive, tenderhearted male who wears his insecurity as a badge of honor. We have veered back and forth between those alternatives for most of our adult lives. Now, if the polls are correct, all of us are compared to Mel Gibson, the macho-sensitive, cocky-insecure cop with cocker-spaniel eyes, an Olympic body, and a lethal weapon.

Somewhere amid the clutter of the paste-up visual stereotypes, in some rare moment of silence, each of us must ask who we really are. If we are to be whole persons, we must discover the real person, the genuine article, the one-and-only, all-time-original person God created us to be.

A recent conversation confirmed this identity struggle in which we mid-life men are involved. At a neighborhood social gathering, one couple told a hilarious story of their recent debacle in attempting to have work done on their car.

A single woman, surprised that the husband had not been able to repair the car himself, said, "I thought all men knew how to fix cars." Immediately, three other men, all of whom appeared to have a healthy sense of their own masculinity, responded that they didn't know the first thing about car repair and didn't intend to learn.

One of them turned to the single woman and asked sarcastically, "Don't all women know how to cook?"

In a perfect world, we would settle the issue of who we are during adolescence. But in this imperfect world, where boys often are encouraged to plow through adolescence without asking the difficult questions, many of us find ourselves at mid-life, asking, "Who am I?" We look at that stranger's face on our driver's license and feel a nagging sense that we have fulfilled external roles but have not resolved the deepest inner questions of our souls. If we take the search seriously, something might awaken within us to offer the hope of new life.

The Living Dead

I was fascinated with the story of a young idealistic doctor who took a position in a charity hospital because he could not find work anywhere else. He was assigned to a floor full of walking zombies, the living dead. Their bodies were alive, but the persons inside were asleep, totally unresponsive to anything around them. Most had been this way for thirty years, consigned to this medical purgatory to be maintained until they died. No one could help them; no one expected anything to change.

But this unusually sensitive doctor, played in the movie *Awakenings* by Robin Williams, began experimenting with massive doses of the drug L-Dopa. If you saw the movie, you remember that unforgettable scene when, one by one, the patients began to awaken after thirty years of sleep. Watching that scene was like watching the flag being raised at the Olympics: If you could watch it without a lump in your throat or a tear in your eye, you'd better check your pulse to make sure you're still alive!

That scene comes back to my mind when I read Paul's staggering affirmation: "But God, who is rich in mercy, out of the great love with which he loved us even when we were dead through our trespasses, made us alive together with Christ" (Eph. 2:4-5).

Paul says that we are like those patients: walking corpses, the living dead. We walk, we talk, we eat, we can perform most of the normal, animal functions of life, but inside, down in the depths of the human personality where it really matters, we are spiritually dead, emotionally inert, unresponsive to the movement of God's Spirit in our lives and our world. "All of us were like them and lived according to our natural desires, doing whatever suited the wishes of our own bodies and minds" (2:3 GNB). We are not bad or evil; we are just normal human beings, living up to the world's expectations, following our normal human cravings and desires: eating, sleeping, fighting, mating, striving for human success, struggling to achieve domination or power, satisfied if our selfish desires are met and frustrated when they are not.

That's who we are. Then somewhere along the way, we begin to sense that there might be more to living than mere existence. We begin to discover the God who, "out of the great love with which he loved us" can make us "alive together with Christ." The most shocking discovery of all is that this coming alive is not accomplished by our energy, our efforts, or our hard work, but by God's grace: "By grace you have been saved through faith, and this is not your own doing; it is the gift of God" (2:8).

In her biography, *An American Childhood*, Annie Dillard, who won the Pulitzer Prize for *Pilgrim at Tinker Creek*, describes one of the most important lessons she has learned: "What is important is anyone's coming awake . . . the moment of opening a life, and feeling it touch—with an electric hiss and cry—this speckled mineral sphere, our present world" (p. 248).

Psychologist Mark Gerzon says that one of his major discoveries revealed that the rules for the second half of life are different from those for the first half: "The rules of the first half are by and large inherited, while the rules of the second half are ones we have to discover for ourselves, anew." He describes his realization that during the first half, his life was focused externally. His identity was based on how other people accepted, evaluated, or responded to him. Coming into mid-life, he realized "that there is something going on inside, and that I'd been so busy watching the movie going on around me that I didn't pay attention to the inner story." What really matters in our struggle to find our own identity is the opening of a life, coming alive, awakening to the life that God offers us in our creation and rouses within us in Jesus Christ.

Awakening to New Life

But how do we awaken to new life? The biblical answer is that it can happen almost anywhere, almost anytime, in almost an infinite variety of ways. Just look at some of the people in the Gospels.

Nondescript shepherds on a Palestinian hillside catch the hint of an angel's song. Something in their slumbering souls awakens to the possibility that a Savior has been born, and they say to one another, "Let's go and find the child."

Anonymous wise men, astrologers, possibly coming from what we now call Iraq, catch a glimpse of a star, the promise of a new ruler, a new kingdom coming into this old world, and they pack up their camels and head off to find him.

Ordinary fishermen, day laborers, mending their nets beside the sea, hear a stranger say, "Follow me, and I will make you fish for people" (Matt. 4:19). Something within them awakens to the possibility that there is more to life than just making a living. They leave their nets and follow Jesus to places they never would have chosen to go.

A Samaritan woman, the victim of prejudice and sexual injustice, meets Jesus beside a well. To her great surprise, he offers her living water so that she will never thirst again, and she runs off, telling everybody she knows about this man who really understands who she is.

A teacher of the law named Nicodemus comes to Jesus with his philosophical doubts and theological questions, and goes away feeling born again, born anew, born to new life by the Spirit of God.

A woman caught in the act of adultery hears Jesus say, "I do not condemn you," and she goes to sin no more.

A penny-pinching, greedy little capitalist named Zaccheus invites Jesus home for dinner and discovers the freedom that comes only when we learn to give.

Not one of those people was perfect. In fact, the last thing they cared about was hiding what the world would call their imperfections. The one thing they had in common was that they could say: "God, who is rich in mercy, out of the great love with which he has loved us . . . made us alive with Christ."

It can happen almost anywhere, almost anytime, to almost anyone, when the light of God's grace breaks into the darkness of our sleeping souls.

I remember the faces of men with whom I've walked the road of mid-life transition, and I think about how they awakened to the new life God had for them.

It happened for one when, weary with the stale inertia that had settled in around him, he was awakened by the compassion of Jesus and his heart was touched as he served food to women and children in a homeless shelter.

It happened for another when, faced with a mandatory early retirement from a major corporation, he sensed that God was calling him to use his business skills in the global mission of the church.

It happened for another when, confused by the demands and expectations that the world was pressing upon him, he began to ask exactly what he wanted from life and entered into a serious reevaluation of his priorities.

The awakening came for another when he became so weary of his attempts to measure up to an artificial, cardboard image of masculinity that he stopped all his hyperactivity, dropped his membership in the health club, and experienced the quiet power of sitting on his back porch with his wife and children.

It happened for still another when he finally acknowledged the truth and began his journey through the twelve steps of Alcoholics Anonymous.

The important thing is waking up to the grace of God, which accepts us just the way we are, in spite of our imperfections. "What really matters is the moment of opening a life and feeling it touch—with an electric hiss and cry—this speckled mineral sphere, our present world." It's like suddenly realizing that God really loves the person whose face is on our driver's license, and that we can love ourselves.

He Said/She Said

Jim: This business of attempting to live up to some external image of manhood—do you think it's the same for women?

Marsha: Sure. Look at all the cosmetic commercials and the way we try to make ourselves attractive. All of us are supposed to look like the models in the magazine ads. Frankly, women have been struggling with the "image" issue a lot longer than men.

Jim: Yes, I guess wishing we looked like Mel Gibson is a newer phenomenon for us. Men have become more image conscious in recent years. So how do we help one another deal with this?

Marsha: First we have to become comfortable with who we are inside. It doesn't mean we are going to stop looking our best, but even plastic surgeons can't change what a person is on the inside. We have to be comfortable with who we are in order to be helpful to one another.

Jim: The goal is to discover the persons God created us to be. How can we help each other move toward that kind of awakening?

Marsha: This is one I have to struggle with because I'm honest enough to admit that I am attracted to "beautiful people," just like everyone else is. I'm mature enough to know that we have to accept people for what they are, not on the basis of their physical appearance, but I also know that it is sometimes difficult to get past those first impressions. There aren't very many Christie Brinkleys in the world, but I'd sure like to be one once in a while. But I find that once I really get to know people, I don't think much about their physical appearance. One of the keys is genuinely coming to appreciate who that person is.

Jim: How can spouses help each other move toward a spiritual "awakening" or discovery?

Marsha: One way is to verbally affirm each other's gifts and describe the beautiful things we see in our partner's life. We can really help build each other's self-esteem. Another way is to explore new experiences together, creating opportunities for new gifts to be awakened. We can also encourage spiritual growth in each other by participating in spiritual retreats, Bible study, or worship—opportunities to grow together spiritually. It won't happen naturally.

Jim: I think the most important thing is also the toughest—namely, to honestly share with each other where we are growing spiritually.

Action Plans for Him and Her

Him/Her: Read the second chapter of Ephesians. Where can you find yourself (your spouse/friend) in this chapter? Have you experienced God's grace in a personal way that is consistent with Paul's description? Discuss your thoughts with your spouse or a friend.

Him/Her: Share your sense of your own identity with your spouse or a friend. Allow that person to respond to your self-description from his or her experience of you.

Him: In your schedule this week, plan to include some specific opportunities for spiritual growth, such as worship, Sunday school, devotional reading and prayer, silent time alone in a sanctuary or chapel that is open on a weekday, and participation in a spiritual growth group.

Her: There are a variety of opportunities for personal awakening and spiritual growth specifically for women. Talk with your pastor or another spiritual leader about groups, books, and other resources that will strengthen your personal identity and spiritual development as a woman. Be open to the witness of women whose experiences are very different from your own. If there is a woman pastor in your community, she may be a helpful guide.

CHAPTER 7

Can You Hear God Laughing?

John 16:20, 22

Very truly, I tell you, you will weep and mourn, but the world will rejoice; you will have pain, but your pain will turn into joy. . . . So you have pain now; but I will see you again, and your hearts will rejoice, and no one will take your joy from you.

There is a simple declarative sentence tucked away in the second psalm, but if we hear what it says about God and about us, it can be a ray of sunlight, breaking into the darkness of our depression like the morning sun breaking over the horizon. The Hebrew poet who heard it reverberating through the heavens said, "He who sits in the heavens laughs" (Ps. 2:4).

Developing an Ear for Laughter

I had suspected the existence of divine hilarity long before I found this biblical confirmation. It began in elementary school the day I learned about the duckbilled platypus. The name alone was enough to tickle my innards. When I saw a picture of this web-footed, duckbilled mammal and learned it was the only mammal that lays eggs, I began to suspect that the Creator must have a wild sense of humor.

Then, when I was still young enough to be convinced that all members of the opposite sex had cooties, I began to figure out the mysteries of conception. Like most prepubescent kids, I think my first giggly reaction was probably, "You've got to be kidding!" I'm glad to report that my understanding of human sexuality has moved beyond that, but when I remember some of the couples I've seen, I'm convinced that some of us fall in love with each other because the Almighty Lover enjoys a good joke.

My adolescent faith was nurtured at an old-time camp meeting that we attended every summer. I was richly blessed by it, but engraved in my memory is the picture of eight or ten of us junior and senior high school kids sitting on a wooden porch one sunny afternoon, laughing, telling stories, and generally having a great time. I will confess that we were not as sensitive as we could have been to the ladies' prayer circle meeting just down the way, because a woman who came along just then quoted to us the Bible verse that says we will be held accountable for every idle word.

Then she asked us, "What would you do if Jesus came back and found you carrying on like this?" I don't remember how we responded, but if I could relive that moment, I would tell her that I would invite him to pull up a rocker and join us, because I'm sure he was already there. In the words of Reinhold Niebuhr:

Humor is concerned with the immediate incongruities of life and faith [is concerned] with the ultimate ones. . . . Laughter is our reaction to immediate incongruities and those which do not affect us essentially. Faith is the only possible response to the ultimate incongruities of existence which threaten the very meaning of life. . . . Humor is, in fact, a prelude to faith; and laughter is the beginning of prayer. In the holy of holies, laughter is swallowed up in prayer and humor is fulfilled by faith.

Hearing God's laughter is a little like having an ear for music. Some folks naturally have perfect pitch; some are simply tone deaf; but most of us can learn to pick up the tune if we give it a try. Once we hear it, once we get an ear for the divine laughter, we can begin to see that the Bible is full of it. In Psalm 2, for instance, the Hebrew poet paints a fantastic word picture.

All the nations are conspiring; all the people of the earth are plotting together; all the kings, all the presidents, and all the people who, by human standards, have power, influence, and authority, are down here scheming, conspiring, and plotting together about how to break God's control of human history. But high up in the heavens, God looks down on their puny plans and laughs.

Laughter is like that: It's often a matter of perspective. The divine hilarity of biblical faith results from seeing human existence from the infinite perspective of the eternal God. One of the transforming experiences during the mid-life journey can be the discovery of that kind of perspective.

Getting the Right Perspective

This line from G. K. Chesterton is now a part of my personal credo for the second half of my life journey: "Angels can fly because they take themselves so lightly." I have become convinced that one clear evidence of human sin, a measure of our lack of trust and faith, is that most of us take ourselves far too seriously. I have lived most of my life with an almost neurotic conviction that what I did really mattered, that my opinion was really important, that nothing was completed until I had put my hand to it. A major part of my own spiritual growth has been learning to take God very seriously, but not to take myself seriously at all; learning to hold onto God very tightly, while holding everything else with a very light—in a sense, playful—touch.

I do not mean to be callously careless about the difficult and demanding issues of the world around us, issues that call forth the best we have to give. I'm not advocating a Pollyanna foolishness that attempts to plaster a syrupy, spiritual smile over the face of real human suffering which, all too often, is the result of human selfishness and sin. I'm not talking about naive religious drivel that grins and says, "God's in heaven and all's right with the world." All is not right with the world, and, as people of the kingdom of God, we are called to do all we can to right the wrongs. But lest we take our own efforts too seriously, this psalm reminds us of the freedom that comes in knowing that God is still God and that we are God's creatures. It celebrates the God who sits in the heavens, which is the biblical image of the absolute authority and ultimate trustworthiness of God.

In his *Companion*, Joseph Campbell wrote these words: "Getting a comedic view of your situation gives you spiritual distance. Having a sense of humor saves you." Then he calls us to "participate joyfully in the sorrows of the world. We cannot cure the world of sorrows, but we can choose to live in joy" (pp. 20, 17).

We are called to live with the sound of divine laughter that comes from trusting in the greatness and goodness of God. But there's a problem here. It's all well and good to laugh, if you are looking down from the rafters of heaven. But what if you are stuck down here in the thick of things? How can we hear the divine laughter when everything goes wrong, when the world closes in on us, when it feels as if God is up there in the heavens, light years removed from the pain and suffering we experience?

Discovering Joy Through Hope

One of Jesus' most stirring reminders of joy is found in John's account of the last supper. I suppose these words would still be true if Jesus had spoken them on the hillside, looking across a sun-soaked valley with the sounds of laughing children in his ears. But he spoke them behind closed doors on the night he was betrayed, with the sounds of an angry mob and voices of vicious politicians echoing in the street. He spoke them with all the political, economic, and religious might of his day in league against him. He spoke them on the way to the cross:

> You will weep and mourn, but the world will rejoice; you will have pain, but your pain will turn into joy. . . . So you have pain now; but . . . no one will take your joy from you. . . . In the world you face persecution. But take courage; I have conquered the world. John 16:20, 22, 33*b*

It's hard to beat the old King James translation of that last verse: "Be of good cheer, for I have overcome the world."

The resonant laughter echoing from heaven is not cheap, shallow, watery frivolity; it is rich, deep, vivid joy. It is gladness that comes from the same place as suffering; joy that comes from the same place as tears. It is the joy of men and women who face the suffering, injustice, and pain of the world in all its fury, but have taken hold of something stronger, deeper, and more powerful. They have grasped the assurance of the ultimate triumph of the goodness of God. They are of good cheer because they know that the power of God in Jesus Christ has overcome the world.

My spiritual growth at mid-life has been profoundly influenced by the Christians of South Africa. Several years ago in Nairobi, Kenya, I heard the divine laughter from the lips of that human elf and spiritual giant, Desmond Tutu. The Archbishop of Capetown and winner of the Nobel Peace Prize has borne on his shoulders the full weight of the suffering and oppression of Apartheid. To hear him speak is to taste the tears, feel the pain of racial prejudice, and share in some small way the suffering of his people. But I heard something else: the lilting laughter, the uproarious joy of one who knows that the power of God in Jesus Christ has already overcome the world. I shall never forget watching him dance for joy with the children of Nairobi at that religious celebration.

Four years later, I visited South Africa just after the release of Nelson Mandela. I heard the stories of men and women who have paid a tremendous price for their witness to the liberating power of the gospel, but I also heard their laughter, their joyful confidence in the ultimate victory of God's kingdom in this world.

But I didn't need to go to Africa to discover this joy. I heard it from one of God's anonymous saints who was the first of many who have shared it with me. I was the guest preacher at a church in another state. We went to visit a woman who was dying of cancer. It had been a tough, terrible time. I asked her what I often ask people in her situation: "What have you learned?" and I was surprised by her response.

A huge smile spread across her pale, hollow face. Her eyes sparkled and her voice danced as she said, "Oh, just one thing: Jesus is Lord!" She had discovered the hope that comes from knowing the One who shares our suffering, experiences our death, and by the power of the resurrection, overcomes the world.

Learning to Laugh

Because I tend to take myself far too seriously, and because I must acknowledge that this kind of laughing-faith does not come naturally for me, I am developing some personal disciplines that help me hear and share in that divine laughter.

First is a disciplined devotional life. When I spend time with God in Bible reading, reflection, and prayer, I find those eternal perspectives that enable me to relax, rest, and trust God in the middle of my overly active life. When I become careless about that devotional discipline, I find myself falling back into that old pattern, with a stress-filled sense that I am responsible for everything. Prayer is tuning our ears to hear the laughter of God.

Second is maintaining free-wheeling friendships. One of the traits I look for in persons who become my closest friends is the ability to make me laugh. I have tried to surround myself with people who can see the silly side of life and who enable me to laugh at myself.

Third, I schedule time for relaxation and entertainment. I need to break free from my responsibilities to see a "useless" movie, to exercise and relax, to go to a football game, or to enjoy a television sit-com with my wife.

One of the most important discoveries I'm making is that when I learn to take myself lightly, I can hear the laughter of God! And you can, too!

He Said/She Said

Jim: How do you feel about this chapter?
Marsha: Just do it! Make me laugh! I mean, it's one thing to talk about this kind of subject; it's another to live it.

Jim: Since we've already acknowledged that laughter and relaxation are needed by overachievers, how have we worked on this together?

Marsha: I take some responsibility for that. I'm a serious person, a rule-follower, a task-oriented person, but I really enjoy people who make me laugh. Because we are both hard-working and serious-minded, it's hard for us to generate that kind of laughter for each other. This means that it's been important for us to build friendships with people who have that gift and can set it free in us. And it also reminds me of Psalm 30:5, which says that "joy comes with the morning." When you go through pain, God helps you laugh again.

Jim: Because we come at things so differently, you don't seem to "get into" my theological analysis of laughter growing out of faith, do you?

Marsha: No. I just laugh because I'm happy, because I'm enjoying the moment. I really don't sit around and think about it. That takes all the fun out of it. Trying to analyze why we laugh is like trying to analyze a kiss. You just have to enjoy it. I think laughter is a gift from God, who is the giver of every gift of joy. That's not to say that I don't agree with what you say, but I'd rather just do it than discuss why we do it.

Jim: Then that's a great place for us to begin laughing together!

Action Plans for Him and Her

Him/Her: Write your responses to these questions and then share them with your spouse or a friend.

- What is your working definition of the word *joy*?
- Where do you find joy in your life?

- What people and things make you joyful?
- What are some of the things you do that bring joy to others?

Him/Her: With your spouse or friend, make a list of things you enjoy doing together. Include things as simple as talking about the most pleasant part of your day to activities that require some advance planning. Try to enjoy at least one planned activity together each week, and fill your days with as many "simple" shared joyous experiences as possible.

Him/Her: Look up the following references in the Bible and find one that speaks to where you are in your personal journey (or your journey with your spouse/friend): Job 33:23-28; Psalm 30; Psalm 51:1-9; Psalm 126; John 16:20-24; Galatians 5:22. Write that verse on a card you can carry in your pocket every day this week.

CHAPTER 8

No One Goes to Heaven Alone

John 15:15

*I do not call you servants any longer . . .
I have called you friends.*

Thomas Merton, the contemplative Trappist monk who was, for a time, a hermit in the Kentucky hills at the Abbey of Gethsemani, said, "No man goes to heaven alone." I've learned that he is correct. Wherever we are headed, the trip is better if we share it with a friend.

Merton learned that lesson as a student at Columbia University. In *The Seven Storey Mountain*, he writes:

Strangely enough, it was on this big factory of a campus that the Holy Ghost was waiting to show me the light. . . . And one of the chief means . . . through which he operated, was human friendship. . . . God brought me and a half a dozen others together . . . and made us friends, in such a way that our friendship would work powerfully to rescue us from the confusion and the misery in which we had come to find ourselves. (pp. 177-78)

Jonathan Dickinson State Park on the Florida coast is as far south from Columbia as you can get, but the Holy

Ghost waited there for me as he had waited for Merton in New York. I remember walking down a sandy path and sitting on a deserted dock one moonlit night. I was there to lead a prayer retreat for a small group of pastors, but something else happened. I gave up being the "leader" and became a brother. We dared to open the private door of our souls to one another, and God made us friends.

A decade later, what began as a one-time retreat is a biannual event. We are very ordinary men who share an extraordinary friendship. Some of our times together have included gut-wrenching pain as one or more of us struggled with some personal anguish. Some of us have stretched our minds as we have wrestled with theology or issues of ministry. A few have been downright dull because we were "brain dead" from the demands of our careers. The consistent elements have been our laughter, honesty, and care for one another. God has made us friends and has used our friendships to strengthen, direct, heal, and restore our souls.

In his last conversation with his disciples before going to the cross, Jesus said, "I do not call you servants any longer . . . I have called you friends" (John 15:15). I am convinced that genuine, down-to-earth, flesh-and-blood friendship may be the most overlooked Christian virtue, the most ignored ministry of the Spirit, and the most neglected means of grace, particularly for men at mid-life.

The dismal descriptions of our male aversion to intimate friendships fill chapters in every book I've seen from the "men's movement." Rather than restate the obvious, I want to describe the kind of friendship Jesus modeled, the kind of friendship he invites his disciples to share, the kind of friendships that have helped me along the way.

Aristotle, who lived three hundred years before Jesus, is not usually considered a Christian philosopher, but the more I've reflected on his three components of friendship, the more Christ-like they seem.

Friends Are People Whose Company We Enjoy

First, Aristotle said that friends are people whose company we enjoy. When I name my closest friends, I am aware that one thing they all have in common is that they make me smile when they come through the door.

Novelist William Styron, the author of *Sophie's Choice*, was the featured speaker at the gathering where his friend, Philip Roth, received the National Arts Club's Medal of Honor for Literature. He told the story of a day he and Roth spent in Dublin, Ireland, looking for some good clean fun, which, he said, was the only kind of fun they could find in Dublin. Nothing turned out the way they planned. It drizzled all day. They went to an expensive hotel for dinner and endured "a long, vile meal of potatoes and gristle." Then Styron said of his friend: "What made the experience more than tolerable, even exhilarating, was Philip's presence on the scene, his ability to convert these ghastly dead ends and moments of existential insult into an episode of both genuine gravity and high hilarity. It was one of the truly memorable days of my life, and among the most richly enjoyed."

The disciples must have said the same thing about Jesus. Walking beside the seashore, telling stories on the hillside, laughing at a dinner party, pouring wine at a wedding, weeping beside a best friend's grave—just his presence on the scene could convert the ordinary disappointments and the ghastly dead ends of life into moments of genuine vitality, moments alive with the freshness of eternal life.

One of my clergy cronies was my roommate for a college glee-club tour many years ago. The trip was crowded, with too many people in too many places in too few days. During our only open afternoon, we were sitting on a bench in a huge shopping mall when we saw several other glee-club members at a distance. When I started to wave them over, my friend said, "Don't do that; I really need some time to myself." When I offered to leave him alone, he replied, "That's okay; I feel as if I can be alone with you." It was one of the best compliments I have ever received. I can say the same thing about him. Friends are people who make a difference not because of what they do or say, but by simply being there.

Friends Are People We Help and People Who Help Us

Second, Aristotle said that friends are people we help and people who help us. In the second letter to his friends in Corinth, Paul described the reciprocal nature of Christian friendship: God "helps us in all our troubles, so that we are able to help others who have all kinds of troubles, using the same help that we ourselves have received" (II Cor. 1:4 GNB).

A Sunday school teacher went around the class asking the children how they felt about Jesus. One child said, "If I asked Jesus if he loved me, he probably wouldn't answer me. He would just send me another kid to play with. He does things like that." When we're in trouble, when we feel absolutely and utterly alone, when we walk through the valley of the shadow and desperately need to know that God is still with us, God usually sends a friend. Jesus does things like that.

I was in the final stages of work on this book when I received the call to leave the suburban congregation I had loved for thirteen years and move to a century-old urban congregation in a city I had only visited a few times. It became official two months later at the denominational conference where changes in pastoral appointments are announced. In spite of all our preparation, there was an emotional jolt to see another preacher's name printed beside the name of "my" church. I was seated with the woman who, after four years as my associate pastor, had become a trusted friend. After the benediction, we parted quickly, without attempting to speak. I headed for the door, where I ran into several people from my new church, who again welcomed me with warmth and love. Feeling strangely torn between a past I deeply loved and a future I could not know, I stepped out into the blazing sun. And there, waiting for me, was one of those brothers from the solstice retreats. I had walked through the valley with him in the past, and he was waiting to walk with me, the gift of God's grace.

Jesus does things like that. Friends are people we help and people who help us.

Friends Are People with Whom We Share a Moral Vision

Third, Aristotle said that friends are people with whom we "share a moral vision," the way Jonathan and David shared a common soul (I Sam. 18:1-5).

My personal favorite in the pantheon of "founding fathers" for this nation is Thomas Jefferson. Near the end of his life, he received a letter from fellow-revolutionary John Adams. They had been friends, then they had been alienated for some time, and now their friendship had been restored. Jefferson's reply to Adams is recorded in *Jefferson Himself* by Bernard Mayo:

A letter from you . . . carries me back to the times when, beset with difficulties and dangers, we were fellow-laborers in the same cause, struggling for what is most valuable. . . . Laboring always at the same oar, with some wave ever ahead threatening to overwhelm us, and yet passing harmless under our bark, we knew not how we rode through the storm with heart and hand, and made a happy port. . . . No circumstances have lessened . . . for one moment my sincere esteem for you, and I now salute you with unchanged affections and respect. (pp. 295-96)

Adams and Jefferson were fellow-laborers in a common cause, bound together in the moral vision that gave birth to this nation. In a similar sense, Jesus said, "I do not call you servants any longer, because the servant does not know what the master is doing; but I have called you friends, because I have made known to you everything that I have heard from my Father" (John 15:15).

Jesus shared with his disciples—and he shares with us—the vision and promise of the Kingdom: the rule, the will, the purpose of God. Christian friends are bound together in Jesus' vision of that Kingdom. They pray for and dare to live as if they believe that God's rule of wholeness, justice, freedom and peace is being fulfilled on earth as it is in Heaven.

Peter Storey is serving the church in Southern Africa. His wife, Elizabeth, was Archbishop Desmond Tutu's secretary when he led the South African Council of Churches. Their son, Alan, is preparing to follow his father and grandfather in the ministry. I've stayed in their home; they have stayed in ours. We are friends. In many ways our lives are different. They are ten thousand miles away. They confront incorrigible evil and suffering. They witness with a courage I can only begin to comprehend. But we are bound together by the vision of God's rule, God's justice, God's peace, God's kingdom coming on earth, and no circumstances of time or geography can separate us from the common vision we share in Jesus Christ.

Second only to my wife and daughters, the most valuable resource for healing, strength, and wholeness in my mid-life journey has been the gift of friendship. Merton said that no man goes to heaven alone. Even if I could, I don't think I'd enjoy the trip.

He Said/She Said

Jim: In the chapter, I mention my group of friends. How have you felt about my running off with them twice a year?

Marsha: I think it's been good for you. You really seem to enjoy getting together with the guys. Frankly, I sometimes think you sound like a bunch of adolescent schoolboys, but I guess that's part of what you enjoy about it!

Jim: Have you ever felt threatened by those relationships?

Marsha: I would feel threatened if I thought you were breaking confidences with me in what you share with them, but I can trust you and your respect for our relationship. Beyond that, I'm glad you have a bunch of cronies who will listen.

Jim: How does this kind of sharing with friends work for women?

Marsha: I think it's different for different women. In general, society has allowed us to be more open in sharing our feelings with one another than it has for men. I know women who love to go off with the "girls" for a weekend, just like you go with the guys. On the other hand, I'm the kind of person who is more comfortable with a few very close friends who share together individually. I guess I'm not the "group" kind.

Jim: You also enjoy friendships with men.

Marsha: Yes. Frankly, I sometimes find women-only

groups to be boring. I really enjoy being with men and with other couples. Does that ever threaten you?

Jim: No, because we have developed the kind of trust you described above. I'm grateful for my male friendships because I did not have many "buddies" when I was growing up; but like you, I really enjoy our friendships with couples in which all of us participate.

Marsha: I'm very intentional about friendships. They don't happen overnight, and they take a lot of care.

Jim: That's right. I have learned that lesson from a few good friends who have been very intentional in maintaining their contact with me. If too many days go by without contact, they call to "check in." From them, I've learned the importance of taking care of relationships so that they can grow, like a well-cared-for plant, by careful watering, fertilizing, and labor.

Action Plans for Him and Her

Him: Read the story of the soul-friendship between David and Jonathan in First Samuel 18:1-5. How does it impress you? Are you comfortable with the intimacy of that relationship? Have you ever had a friend like that or been that kind of friend to someone else? Discuss your thoughts with your spouse or friend, if you choose.

Him: In one column, list the names of the persons you consider your closest friends. In another column, list the elements that characterize each friendship, using Aristotle's three elements of friendship as a guide. Think about what changes you need to make in your life in order to develop stronger friendships.

Him/Her: How do you feel about your spouse or friend spending time with friends? Share your feelings in nonaccusatory language (i.e., use "I" language rather than "you" language). Discuss ways that each of you might cultivate other friendships without neglecting your own relationship.

Her: Schedule a lunch or "phone visit" with your most trusted female friend. Share with her how your husband's (friend's) mid-life experience is affecting you, without breaking any confidences with your husband (friend). Covenant to pray together as you move through this process.

Her: Name the three or four persons you trust most deeply. How did these relationships develop? Do any of these relationships need to be renewed or strengthened? Make a "plan of action" for nurturing these and other friendships.

Things You Didn't Learn in the Boys' Locker Room

Song of Songs 4:10 GNB

Your love delights me,
my sweetheart and bride.
Your love is better than wine;
your perfume more fragrant than any spice.

Our excursion through the mid-life experience has finally arrived at the stop which dominates so much of what we hear and read about men at mid-life: Sex!

I've already divulged that I by-passed the detour marked "Infidelity: Get it while you can!" The "other" in whom I hoped to find self-worth and with whom I was tempted to break my marriage vow was not some gorgeous young woman. The "other" in my life was my career.

My liberation process included being set free from my love affair with my career. My mistress was the church. But while I am sure that I am not alone in that temptation, the focus of this chapter is on liberation from the often distorted, and sometimes destructive, sexual assumptions that most of us "inherited" from our parents, learned in the locker room, explored in the backseat of a Chevy, or acquired from the male-dominated culture in which we grew up. Part of our task at mid-life is to move toward a healthier, more mature understanding of sexuality that we can enjoy for the rest of our lives.

Let me pause here to say that this chapter is not written for persons who have been sexually abused or harassed, or for persons who have cheated or been cheated. It is for basically "healthy" people who want to find a stronger, healthier, more distinctively Christian understanding of their sexuality. My hope is to help men—and thereby the women in their lives—who have grown up surrounded by those distorted assumptions find new ways of understanding their sexuality.

I know of no better place to begin than with that marvelous Old Testament love poem known as the Song of Solomon, though the Hebrew is more accurately translated as "The Song of Songs." The Good News Bible introduces it as "The most beautiful of songs, by Solomon." The Living Bible paraphrases it to read, "The Song of Songs, more wonderful than any other." It is a lyrical, passionate, erotic celebration of sexual love and intimacy. With the music of that Song in the background, let me share three ideas that can help us move toward a mature, Christian understanding of our sexuality.

The Search for Intimacy

First is an understanding of human sexuality as a search for intimacy within a relationship based on a covenant of trust and loyalty, rather than a search for intimacy with a sexual partner. In one segment of the television series "Saint Elsewhere," a young, good-looking, promiscuous male intern began to seduce the teenage daughter of one of the surgeons. When his fellow-intern questioned the relationship, he said he was not looking for relationships, just receptacles. His graphic imagery was a ruthlessly honest description of a male understanding of sexuality entirely focused on sexual satisfaction through intercourse.

The alternative is to see our sexual desire as an expression of our deeper desire for human intimacy. Sexual intercourse is one expression of that desire, but not the only one. Seen in that perspective, the awareness of a possible decline of sexual prowess in the later years need not destroy a man's sense of masculinity or drive him, panic stricken, into the bed of a younger woman.

The Song of Solomon is joyfully erotic and profoundly sensual. With no hesitation, fear, or embarrassment, the woman sings:

> Your lips cover me with kisses;
> your love is better than wine.
> There is a fragrance about you;
> the sound of your name recalls it . . . .
> My lover has the scent of myrrh.
> 1:1-3b, 13a GNB

> His face is bronzed and smooth . . . .
> His body is like smooth ivory,
> with sapphires set in it.
> His thighs are columns of alabaster
> set in sockets of gold. . . .
> His mouth is sweet to kiss;
> everything about him enchants me.
> 5:11a, 14b-15a, 16a GNB

And the man sings to the woman:

> How beautiful you are, my love!
> How your eyes shine with love behind your veil.
> Your hair dances like a flock of goats . . . .
> Your teeth are as white as sheep
> that have just been shorn and washed. . . .

> Your love delights me,
>   my sweetheart and bride.
> Your love is better than wine;
>   your perfume more fragrant than any spice.
> The taste of honey is on your lips . . . .
> Your clothing has all the fragrance of Lebanon.
>   4:1-2, 10-11 GNB

Now, that's sensual, which means that it delights the senses. But it goes beyond mere physical pleasure. The entire poem exudes a profound sense of soul-intimacy which includes and celebrates a physical relationship, but is not limited to it. Couples who discover that kind of soul-intimacy will mature into geriatric lovers for whom the wink of an eye can be as sensual as a kiss.

The journey toward sexual maturity begins when we are able to understand our sexual desire as the search for intimacy within a relationship bound by a covenant of trust and loyalty, rather than a search for sexual partners. The second step along this path is to move from the ambition for mastery to the acceptance of mystery.

The Acceptance of Mystery

While I am grateful for the openness that has come in the wake of the sexual revolution, the freedom to talk about the "how" of sexual intercourse can become an overemphasis on technique, or the mastery of skills, so that sexual satisfaction depends upon performance, denying the inherent mystery of this complex part of the image of God in our humanity. If we are "mysteriously and wonderfully" made, I can think of no other part of our human personalities that is more mysterious or wonderful than our common sexuality.

Don't forget that the first miracle, the first evidence of what John called the "glory of God" in Jesus, was a very sensual miracle at a wedding feast (John 2:1-10). The wine ran out. Their lips were parched; their throats were dry. Jesus took water—colorless, odorless, tasteless, stale from sitting in the vessels—and transformed it into wine. When the dinner host tested it, let it run over his tongue, he exclaimed, "Ah! You have saved the best wine for the last!"

The story delights the senses. It is an expression of the miraculous beauty of God's love in human life. It is mystery because no matter how closely we study the technique, we can never fully comprehend how it happened.

The same could be said for human sexuality. Each of us needs to learn the skills, the ways of romance and sexual behavior that can give pleasure to our marriage partner. I remind the couples I counsel that in order to get a driver's licence, one must study the manual. The least they can do for each other is to read a good book on sex. But when we have mastered the technique, we have not begun to experience the marvelous mystery of personhood that is inherent in the sharing of our sexuality.

When Goethe first heard Bach's "Well-tempered Clavier," he said it sounded "as if the ethereal harmony were communing with itself, as might have happened in God's bosom shortly before the creation of the world." The maturity toward which two people move in their shared sexuality is the kind of "ethereal harmony" which the Father, Son, and Holy Spirit share in the mystery of the Trinity, the harmony that gave birth to the whole creation.

If that is difficult to comprehend, I encourage you to compare the dancing of young adults, scattered almost anonymously around the dance floor, with the elegant perfection of an older couple dancing together. There may be passion in the first, but there is maturity in the second, the kind of mystical, musical maturity that comes only from long years of harmony together.

A Lifelong Commitment

The transitions I've described so far are parts of a larger transition—from sex as immediate experience to human sexuality as timeless, faithful commitment. Precisely because it is such a marvelous gift, precisely because it is such a profound reflection of the image of God in our being, the Bible calls us to handle our sexual relationships very carefully, in a covenant of trust and loyalty.

My wife and I celebrated our twentieth wedding anniversary on the island of Bermuda. Like most tourists who visit the town of St. George's, we climbed the stairs to St. Peter's Church, the oldest site of continuous Anglican worship in the Western hemisphere, dating back to the discovery of the islands in the early 1600s. When you enter the building, the first thing you see is a stone baptismal font over five hundred years old. It came from England with the first settlers and is still used today to celebrate God's love for us in the sacrament.

On weekdays, when gawking tourists stumble off the tour buses and through the church, a velvet rope is placed around the font. When it is not being used for its intended purpose, it is off limits, protected from abuse or careless disregard.

Biblical faith puts some velvet ropes, moral fences, around our sexual relationships, not because biblical people ever thought sex was dirty, vile, or sinful, but solely because we believe it is such a marvelous gift of God. Sex is not intended for use as a party game, a means of manipulation, or for merchandizing soap, automobiles, or anything else.

Along with its open sensuality, the Song of Solomon contains an element of privacy, a careful protection of this intimate relationship between the man and woman. She sings:

> Take me with you, and we'll run away;
> be my king and take me to your room.
>
> 1:4a GNB

He sings:

> Come then, my love;
> my darling, come with me.
> My sweetheart, my bride, is a secret garden,
> a walled garden, a private spring.
>
> 2:10b, 4:12 GNB

Biblical faith believes that the intimacy and mystery of our sexuality is intended for fulfillment in a lifelong covenant of trust and love.

In Thornton Wilder's drama *The Skin of Our Teeth,* a man named George comes back from the war to his wife, Maggie, only to tell her that he wants to leave her for another woman. Maggie has a few words for him: "I married you because you gave me a promise. . . . That promise made up for your faults. And the promise I gave you made up for mine. Two imperfect people got married, and it was the promise that made our marriage."

When George replies that the war has changed him, she answers, "Oh, George, you have to get it back again. Think! What else kept us alive all those years? Even now, it's not comfort we want. We can suffer whatever's necessary; only give us back the promise." George eventually realizes what it is that keeps life together and renews the promise.

Am I maintaining that there is no place for divorce and that every married couple must, of necessity, stick together? No. Some couples have all the intimacy of two cats in a burlap bag. For some, the mistake was the marriage, and healing can come only through separation and a new beginning. But I've seen enough couples go through the pain of a broken relationship to believe that we need to focus our attention on the importance of the promise and lift up the possibility of renewal. I have seen enough couples work through their pain and pay the price for healing to know that it can be done, and that the new relationship can be deeper, richer, and healthier than the original one.

In an interview, psychologist Mark Gerzon was asked what it means for mid-life couples to "fall out of love." He responded:

> Some people wake up in bed next to somebody they've been married to for years, feel like they're with a stranger, and think, "Well, this must be the time to get divorced." Fortunately, my wife, Shelley, and I went through that crisis and found that the person we were with was far more interesting than the projection we had when we were young. . . . My wife and I found, after almost 20 years, that we are now free to be ourselves with each other in a way that we had never been before.

Broken relationships can sometimes be healed. The process can, in fact, liberate us from our past and enable us to discover new possibilities for ourselves and our spouses.

A Reflection of Divine Love

The Song of Songs leaves one more mile marker along the road to sexual maturity. The Hebrew love poem has often been interpreted allegorically, as a picture of the love of God for Israel and the love of Christ for the Church. It points to the divine love of which our human passion is a pale reflection. We dare to believe that just as we love and are loved in the intimacy of our sexual relationships, we can love and be loved by God, the Infinite Lover who woos us, calls us, invites us to know the divine love in our own experience.

The Hebrew word *ydh*—in English, "to know"—is used interchangeably in scripture to speak of knowing God or knowing another person in sexual intercourse. And isn't there something deep within each of us that longs to cry out to God with the words of Solomon, "My beloved is mine and I am his" (2:16*a* GNB)? Wouldn't you like to sing of your relationship with God as the poet did?

> He brought me to his banquet hall
> and raised the banner of love over me.
> 2:4 GNB

In his work included in *The English Spirit*, John Donne, England's great poet and preacher of the seventeenth century, attempted to combine the spiritual reality of his relationship with God with the passion and power of sexual love. It's "olde" English, but I think you can capture the feeling of it:

> Batter my heart, three person'd God; for, you
> As yet but knocke, breathe, shine and seeke to mend;
> That I may rise, and stand, o'erthrow mee, and bend
> Your force, to breake, blowe, burn and make me new. . . .
> Yet dearely I love you, and would be loved faine,
> But am betroth'd unto your enemie;
> Divorce mee, untie, or break that knot againe,
> Take mee to you, imprison mee, for,
> Except you enthrall mee, I never shall be free,
> Nor ever chast, except you ravish mee. (p. 76)

Amid all the discussion of sexual attitudes, sexual values, and sexual commitments, the one unique word offered by biblical faith is that our sexual love is a reflection of the divine love of God. Once "ravished" by that love, our human loves have an honest-to-goodness chance of becoming "the most beautiful of songs."

He Said/She Said

Jim: Let's talk about how people develop a sense of "soul-intimacy." What does that phrase mean to you?

Marsha: I think it means a deep sense of trust, a feeling of security that enables you to share yourself with another person and know that he or she will understand, value your opinion, and keep your confidence. That kind of understanding can develop to a level at which two people know each other so well that they can communicate a world of feelings with the wink of an eye.

Jim: How do people develop that kind of trust and understanding?

Marsha: Very slowly. It takes lots of time and lots of conversation. You have to talk about everything. You test the waters at first. If trust is broken, you have to come back and work on it together. It means clarifying how you feel and making sure that the other person understands. It also means making lots of mistakes. You have to be willing to accept each other's fumbling attempts and love each other through it.

Jim: Given the sexual sickness and abuse in our society, there is a lot of pain out there.

Marsha: Since I haven't experienced that kind of severely broken trust, I can only speak through my experiences with others and encourage people to be honest about where they are and what they are facing, and to get the best help they can in dealing with it. It is incredibly painful, but as you said, we have seen couples who have found healing and a new relationship.

Action Plans for Him and Her

Him: Are there shadowy places in your life that you need to share with your spouse or a good friend? Are there shadowy corners of your sexual experience that need the penetrating light of the pure love of God in Jesus Christ? Are you carrying damaged or damaging sexual attitudes from your past? Our human sexuality is such a complex part of our personality that this may be the point at which you need the help of a therapist or pastoral counsellor. Be honest enough to find the help you need. Make an appointment with your pastor or another Christian therapist or teacher to determine your need for specific help.

Her: How well do you understand your husband's understanding of human sexuality and sexual relationships? Ask him to share his own story of the people and experiences that have shaped his sexual understandings. Then share your own story with him.

Him/Her: Write a letter to your partner, specifically describing the ways your sexual relationship is satisfying to you and also listing those things that are unpleasant but are usually unspoken.

Him: Take action in expressing your love for your spouse in ways that she will appreciate. Here are some possibilities:

- Surprise her with a romantic greeting card or small gift, just because you love her.

- Take out the garbage, wash the dishes, do the laundry, or perform some other household chore without being asked.
- Commit yourself to giving her an honest compliment each day. This will require you to watch for her best traits and talents expressed in ordinary ways.
- Ask how her day has gone and *really listen!*
- Read together the Song of Solomon. (If you have children, do this alone in a quiet room, after they are asleep!)
- Take her to some event she would enjoy. (Arrange for a baby sitter if you have young children.)

Him/Her: Talk together about how you see your relationship changing in the future. What will it be like for you to grow old together? How will your relationship change as the children leave home—and/or you leave the workplace—and you begin again together? What actions can you take to develop the kind of "soul-intimacy" described in this chapter?

Him/Her: Select a retired-age couple in your community or church family who seem to model the kind of relationship you would like when you are their age. Schedule a visit with them and ask them to share things they have done to maintain their relationship across the years.

Him/Her: Learn to dance, engage in a sport, or participate in a hobby *together*. Attend a marriage enrichment weekend or take a marriage communication class through your church.

Do You Need a Good Vacation?

Luke 10:36-37*b*

*"Which of these three . . . was a neighbor to the
man who fell into the hands of the robbers?" . . .
"The one who showed him mercy." . . .
"Go and do likewise."*

The story of the unfortunate traveler who was attacked by thieves on his way to Jericho is one of the best-known stories Jesus ever told. You don't need to wear a string of perfect attendance pins from Sunday school; you don't need to own a Bible; you don't even need to be religious to recognize the rescuer's name. Just about everyone has heard of the good Samaritan. And that's the problem. We think we already know what the story says.

So let's not begin with the good Samaritan. Let's begin where Luke begins, with a lawyer, a scribe, a student of the law, who asks the question for which the parable of the good Samaritan is the answer.

Searching for Something More

Luke doesn't record the lawyer's name, but I've been doing some research, and I think I've found him, or at least someone a lot like him. I think it's Billy Crystal in the movie *City Slickers*. If you saw the movie, you remember that Billy Crystal played an advertising salesman who, on his thirty-ninth birthday, was experiencing a classic male mid-life crisis. Everything had turned a dull, flat shade of gray. His life had all the zing of a wet tennis ball. His work seemed useless. His patient wife's patience had just about run out. When his two buddies suggested a two-week vacation on a cattle drive out west, his wife told him to go and find his smile.

City Slickers is the kind of movie that hits home because so many of us know exactly what Crystal's character felt. Most of us have been on or would like to go on the kind of vacation that helps us rediscover our smile.

A very successful CPA followed me into my office one night. He slouched down into a chair and said, "Jim, I don't know what's wrong with me. I just got the promotion I always wanted. We have a beautiful home in the best neighborhood. I have a great wife and wonderful kids. I should be the happiest guy around, but I'm so depressed I have to force myself to get out of bed in the morning."

A career woman told me that the biggest problem she and her husband faced was trying to decide which of their toys to play with next, none of which really mattered at all.

I felt it the day I woke up and discovered that I had burned up all my physical and emotional reserves. The tank was empty, the well was dry.

That's the guy in this story found in the Gospel of Luke, the one who came to Jesus and asked the question that is at the center of our mid-life seeking, although most of us would not use his language: "What must I do to inherit eternal life?" (10:25)

Before hearing Jesus' answer, let's be sure we understand the question. The Living Bible paraphrases verse 25 this way: "What does a man need to do to live forever in heaven?" The most obvious problem with this paraphrase is that women ask this kind of question as often as men; but more important, by Luke's account, the question is far more urgent and much more personal. The lawyer asked, "What must *I* do . . . ?"

This was not an objective, philosophical debate about some "man" or some "woman." The question came right out of this guy's guts. It expressed the gnawing hunger in his soul, a deep inner thirst that nothing had been able to quench. If we want to understand Jesus' answer, we need to feel the penetrating power of that question: "What must *I* do . . . ?"

There is a story of a young monk who made a pilgrimage into the forest to see if the wise hermit who lived there could tell him the secret of life. The hermit led him down to the river and out into the middle of the stream. He forced the young man's head under the water and held it there until he came up gasping for breath. Then the hermit said, "When you want life as much as you want air, you'll find it." That was the kind of search that brought this lawyer to Jesus.

The Living Bible paraphrase asks what a person needs to do "to live forever in heaven." That's not a bad question, but it's not the question Luke records here. When the Gospel writers use the term "eternal life," they are not talking about "living forever in heaven." They are not referring to some sort of eternal existence that we discover on the other side of death. "Eternal life" is a *quality* of living, a way of being in relationship with God that begins right here, right now; and it is so vibrant, so alive, so filled with the never-ending life of the Spirit of God, that it can never be put to death. Eternal life includes heaven after death, but it begins right here, right now.

Whether they realized it or not, that's what the vacationing "city slickers" were looking for. They packed their bags and headed west for the cattle drive, led by a rugged, leathery old cowboy played by Jack Parlance. One of the key moments in the movie occurs when Billy Crystal, with a combination of fear and fascination, asks the old cowboy to teach him the secret to life. The cowboy points a tough old finger at Crystal's face and says, "One thing. Just one thing." Excited as a kid on Christmas morning, Crystal asks, "What is it?" Parlance responds, "That's for you to find out."

In one sense, the old cowboy was absolutely correct. Just as no one can take your bath for you, no one can live life for you. Each of us must experience life for ourselves. But the problem with the cowboy's response is that it hooks onto the very thing that gives us so much trouble in the first place—the radical individualism, the narrow self-centeredness of our time. We have been conditioned to think that every question can be answered from the standpoint of our own self-interest, as if there is no truth, no reality, no authority beyond our own feelings; as if the only thing that ultimately matters is what's in it for me. Our generation has proved the truth of A. R. Ammons' poem:

> By the time I got the world cut down small enough
> that I could be the center of it, it wasn't worth having.

Finding Real Life

The lawyer in the Gospel story had enough sense to know that he would never find the full resolution of his deepest needs inside himself. He knew that if anyone, anywhere, any time, had the answer to that question, it had to be Jesus. He asked, "What must I do to find life: real life, life that is so alive with the Spirit of God that it can never be put to death?" And Jesus, like every effective teacher, threw the question back to him: "What do you read in the law?"

This guy was no dummy. He was a good Jew; he had grown up in the synagogue. He knew the correct answer: "You shall love the Lord your God with all your heart, and with all your soul, and with all your strength, and with all your mind; and your neighbor as yourself" (10:27). Jesus said, "You have given the right answer; do this, and you will live" (10:28).

Notice that Jesus did not say, "Believe this and you will live," as if the answer to eternal life could be found in knowing the right doctrine, quoting the appropriate authority, or giving the correct answers on a standardized test. Like those advertisements that tell us to "Just do it!" Jesus was saying, "Do this, live this way, act on this, and you will start living."

Eternal life—life that is so alive with God's Spirit that it can never die—has more to do with living, acting, and being than with merely believing; it is not just intellectual assent to an idea but loving obedience to a living Lord. The one thing that really matters in life is described with an active, imperative verb: "*Love* the Lord your God with all your heart and soul and mind and strength, and *love* your neighbor as yourself." Do this, Jesus instructed, and you'll find life.

Jesus' response evidently penetrated far deeper than the lawyer wanted to go. He had always believed this—he had known it as a religious truth. The problem was in doing it. Luke records one of those fascinating verses that perfectly describes what most of us practice so well: "But wanting to justify himself, he asked Jesus, 'And who is my neighbor?'" (10:29) In response, Jesus tells the story of the man who fell into the hands of robbers.

You know the rest of the story—how the religious folks, the pious folks, the folks with all the right answers, the clean-living folks, kept themselves clean by walking past on the other side of the road. No life there. No Spirit. Just stale, cold, unfeeling religious tradition without a drop of red blood in it.

And you know how the Samaritan, the outcast, the social reject, the one who wasn't allowed inside the Temple wall, stopped, picked the poor man up, bandaged his wounds, dropped him off at the inn, and left his credit card to pay the bill.

And did you notice the way Jesus turned the lawyer's question on its head? The lawyer had asked, "Who is my neighbor?" Jesus queried the lawyer: "Which of these was neighbor—acted in a neighborly way—to the man who fell among thieves?" The lawyer could not avoid the obvious answer: "The one who showed him mercy." And Jesus said, "Go and do likewise" (10:37).

Giving Is Receiving

Do you want to find life, real life, life that is so alive with the Spirit of God that it can never be put to death? Then go and do likewise. Just do it! Love God with all your heart and soul and mind and strength, and start loving—actively loving—other folks the way you love yourself; and then, when you have lost yourself in the self-giving love of Christ, you'll find the one thing that really matters: You'll find eternal life!

Dan Wakefield was a mid-life traveler like a lot of us. Although he was a successful journalist, screenwriter, and novelist, his personal life was a wreck when, one Christmas Eve, he found his way to King's Chapel in Boston. He had not been in church for more than twenty-five years, and he chose King's Chapel from the Boston *Globe* religion pages because it sounded the least threatening.

As he writes in *Returning: A Spiritual Journey*, he assumed that "Candlelight Service" meant "nothing more religiously challenging than carol singing." That inauspicious step marked the beginning of a genuine conversion in his life. "Going to church," he discovered, "even belonging to it, did not solve life's problems—if anything, they seemed to escalate again around that time—but it gave me a sense of living in a larger context, of being part of something greater" (pp. 12, 28).

One of the significant turning points in his journey came on the morning after a long night of personal anguish in the home of a friend:

> I woke the next morning . . . and paced around the house . . . looking at some interesting new posters . . . . The one that seemed to leap out at me was by Albert Schweitzer. . . . The message . . . "spoke to me" in a very clear way, as if I were reading my own instructions in a game that gave me "clues" to my next direction. It said, "I don't know what your destiny will be, but one thing I know, the only ones among you who will be really happy are those who have sought and found a way to serve." (p. 201)

Back in Boston, after Wakefield joined the King's Chapel congregation and became active in its ministries, the members of his church family gave him the most important gift of all: the chance to serve. He says that he responded from "a sort of 'enlightened selfishness'; not because it made me holy but because it made me happy" (p. 227).

That's the lesson Billy Crystal, the city slicker, learns when he is forced to risk himself for the sake of someone (or something) he loves—a calf named Norman—which nearly drowns in a storm-flooded river. From that single act of self-giving, his love expands to his wife and family. He returns to the city, having rediscovered not only his smile, but also the kind of joy that is experienced only when we find a way to give ourselves to others.

The most hopeful sign I see among the now middle-aged idealists of the 1960s is a profound desire to make a difference by serving the needs of the community around them. People are searching for ways to offer their own energy, skill, and time. In offering themselves for others, they are finding a genuine sense of vocation.

After telling the parable of the good Samaritan, Jesus told the young man to "*go and do likewise.*" Luke ends the story there. We will never know what the lawyer did, which leaves the rest of the story up to us.

He Said/She Said

Marsha: You wrote about your discovery that your "tank was empty and your well was dry." Did you find your solution to that problem by finding a way to serve?

Jim: That's a good question. It's not the "serving" part of my career that necessarily drains my energy as much as the "maintenance" part. I am convinced that Billy Crystal's character represents both the way our society is geared toward self-interest and our need to give ourselves to something larger than ourselves. I do "find my smile" in those relationships that reflect the kind of caring and serving I describe here, but I also am learning when to break away to take care of my own soul.

How is it for you? The traditional wife/mother role includes a lot of "serving" directed toward children. How do you find the kind of happiness that comes through serving others?

Marsha: That changed with the girls' ages. When they

were small, you were in your "never say no" stage, so I made a conscious choice to invest myself in the girls. As they grew older, I was able to turn to projects outside the family. There is also a stamina issue here. Some high-energy folks can go in all sorts of directions at one time, while some of us can only do a few things. As a school teacher, the energy I invest in my children at school continues to take most of what I have to give. You have to know what you are able to do and then "Just do it!"

Jim: Do you remember Billy Crystal's wife in *City Slickers*? Did you see anything in her character that models ways wives can be helpful to guys like us?

Marsha: She gives him the freedom to go and find himself. She was lovingly honest in telling him that he wasn't fun anymore, she encouraged him to find what he needed, and she welcomed him home when he came back. There probably isn't enough there to build a role model, but she gives us a good place to start.

One other thing: I remember hoping for one simple solution when the old cowboy held up his finger and said, "One thing," even though I knew it could not be that simple. Each person has to allow others to be original in finding their answer and not expect a carbon copy of the answer they find for themselves, as long as those answers are centered in the kind of love we find in Jesus Christ.

Action Plans for Him and Her

Him: Read Luke 10:25-37 as if you never had heard or read it before. What surprises or offends you? List these things in your journal or notes. Can you identify with any of the characters in the story? Rewrite the story from the perspective of the character with whom you identify.

Him/Her: Rent the video of *City Slickers*. Watch it with your spouse or a friend. See if you can identify with any of the feelings of the characters in the movie. When you do, stop the tape and share that feeling.

Him: Print the Albert Schweitzer quote from this chapter on a card that you can hang on your mirror, carry in your pocket, or tape to the dashboard of your car. Read the quotation each day as a spiritual-mental focus for a week. ("The only ones among you who will be happy are those who have sought and found a way to serve.")

Him: Make a list of ways you can find the happiness that comes only in learning to serve. Ask your pastor for suggestions. Watch for volunteer needs in your community. Then just go do it!

Her: Think about these questions and then make your own "plan of action" for the week or month:

- How can you encourage him to "search for something more" while not neglecting your own needs? In what ways can you assist him in this search?
- What experiences and thoughts of your own can you share that illustrate how you have found happiness through serving others?
- In what constructive ways can you share your own needs and your dissatisfaction with his "wandering"?

Her: What about your own happiness? Have you found a meaningful way to serve? Investigate the needs of local helping agencies supported by your church. Find a place to use your talents outside your own home.

CHAPTER 11

What Will They Say When I'm Gone?

Philippians 3:7, 10-11

Yet whatever gains I had, these I have come to regard as loss because of Christ. . . . I want to know Christ and the power of his resurrection and the sharing of his sufferings by becoming like him in his death, if somehow I may attain the resurrection from the dead.

(While the manuscript for this book was with the publisher, I suddenly found myself hospitalized with a rare and potentially dangerous inflammation in the muscle of my heart. There is nothing like the moment the doctor says, "It's your heart." That will jerk the future into the present! Immediately, I was forced to ask the question of this chapter more directly.

Now on the way to recovery, I must reaffirm both the importance of asking the question and my deepened commitment to the answers, along with profound gratitude for the friendships that have supported us and the peace of Christ which surrounds us.)

What will they say about me when I'm dead and gone? That may seem a strange question at first—not exactly the kind we ask in polite society—but it could change the way we live. What will they say about me?

That can be a difficult dilemma for preachers. The story is told of a preacher who got carried away when giving a eulogy. He described the deceased as a loving husband, a wonderful father, and a great asset to the community. About half way through the eulogy, the widow poked her son and said, "Go take a look in the casket and make sure that's your Pa he's talking about."

If they really tell the truth, what will they say about you?

My wife and I have asked that question in another setting that has nothing to do with death. As we worked at parenting across the years, whenever we were tempted to be critical of our parents, one of us would turn to the other and ask, "What do you think our kids will say about us?" We decided not to leave the answer to chance. We tried to predetermine their responses by living in ways that are consistent with the way we'd like to be remembered later.

What will they say about me? Without being maudlin or morbid, a mid-life look at the end of our lives can become a way of setting priorities and plotting the course of the rest of our trip. Although I am sure the answers will continue to be refined by the opportunities and experiences that come my way, several elements remain constant. I share my response in the hope that it will encourage you to develop your own.

Following Jesus

First, I hope people will say that I was a follower of Jesus Christ. The motto of the church youth group I attended as an adolescent was "Christ Above All." It wasn't a bad place to begin; it wouldn't be a bad place to end; and it is a great way to live. I'd like to be remembered as a person who attempted to bring every inch of human experience under the influence of the words, way, and Spirit of Jesus.

Paul expressed that desire in his autobiographical letter

to the Philippians. Looking back across all he had done, all he had experienced, all he had suffered, all he had learned, all he had lost, he said there was one thing he wanted more than anything else: "Whatever gains I had, these I have come to regard as loss because of Christ" (3:7). Another version translates it this way: "All those things that I might count as profit I now reckon as loss for Christ's sake" (3:7 GNB).

In one sense, everything had become very simple for Paul. His priorities were clear. Above everything else, he wanted to know Christ, share his suffering for the world, and become like him, even in death, in the hope of sharing with him in the resurrection.

In reevaluating my personal priorities, I am finding that in some ways things are becoming simpler for me. When I look at my life from the perspective of its end, the desire to live as a growing, honest, genuine disciple of Jesus Christ immediately takes priority over everything else.

One example of how this desire to follow Jesus has taken shape in my life is my growing commitment to Jesus' way of nonviolence and peace. My generation came through adolescence during the Vietnam era which unmasked the demons of our nation's warring psyche. Many of my idealistic peers marched in the peace movement.

I regret that I did not march for peace. But since those days, I have moved in the direction of nonviolence revealed in Jesus and modeled by Ghandi, Martin Luther King, Jr., Archbishop Desmond Tutu, and a host of lesser-known saints. Being far removed from mere sociopolitical conviction, I am discovering the way of nonviolence that grows out of a deep spirituality, centered in the love of God and the scandal of the cross (see I Cor. 18-25).

The desire to follow Jesus' way of peace immediately

forces me to spiritual discipline in prayer, the primary means by which we nurture the way of Jesus within us. It also has led me to a deeper sense of compassion in sharing the honest hurt of those around me, a stronger commitment to social justice, and a more vibrant sense of Christian community with my brothers and sisters in Christ. Though I cannot predict all the forms it may take in the future, I am determined to keep following the way of Jesus.

Loving Others

I also hope others will say that I loved people and shared life fully with them. I once heard a motivational speaker in a junior-high assembly say, "People are meant to be loved; things are meant to be used." The great tragedy of our time is that it's so easy to start loving things and using people.

Donald Musser, professor at Stetson University, reflected on his twenty-year battle with cancer:

> This unwanted, unwelcome, dreaded fate has enabled a different person to emerge in me . . . now people and relationships take priority. . . . If I had to live through a major illness again, there is one part . . . I would change. I chose to make my experience with cancer very private. . . . I now consider my previous orientation to have been selfish and stupid. I would now want to be encompassed by a caring community of friends with whom I could share the inner mental and emotional trauma of illness. (*Context*, November 1, 1987, pp. 4-5)

His recommendation to the rest of us: "Embrace your wife and daughter and puppy dog and invite a few friends in to share a moment of *l'chaim*."

115

Enjoying Life

I also hope that when I'm gone someone will say that I loved life and tried to enjoy it. I hope my daughters will remember me as a man who was alive to the mystery, the wonder, and the beauty of the world, a person who threw himself fully into the life he was given to live and who knew how to laugh.

One of our favorite family vacations was a summer trip to Grand Lake, Colorado, on the edge of the Rocky Mountain National Forest. Driving across Ridge Trail one brilliant morning, we had our picture taken at the continental divide, where I remembered a story I had heard years before. It's the tale of a family who planned to drive across the country from Chicago to California. At the last minute, an emergency in the father's business forced him to remain behind. The rest of the family drove on and he planned to meet them in San Francisco.

But the business crisis was resolved more quickly than expected, so unknown to his family, he flew to Denver and arranged for someone to take him out along the highway, so that when the family arrived at the continental divide, he would be standing there, suitcase in hand, thumbing a ride.

When he returned to his office, a co-worker asked why he had gone to so much trouble to do such a crazy thing. The grinning father replied, "One of these days I am going to be gone, and I want my kids to be able to say, 'Dad could be a lot of fun.'"

Living with Passion

I also hope that people will say I lived with passion. Now that I am beginning to get my compulsive behavior under control, I am discovering the freedom to be an unashamed man of passion, with deep, rich emotions born out of convictions that go to the core of my being.

It was the Sunday my sixth-grade daughter was becoming a member of the church. She and the other young people joining the church that day were in the first group that had come through elementary school together in that church family. It was a special time, and I was enjoying the smiles on the kids' faces and the warmth of their church family. Unaware of how deeply I was being moved, I placed my hand on my daughter's head and began to speak the words, "Carrie Lynn Harnish, the Lord defend thee . . . . " But before I could complete her name, a huge lump the size of Texas stuck in my throat. I caught my breath I tried again. I could not speak. For what seemed an interminable span of time, I held back the flow of tears until I could at least say the words, bond over, and whisper in her ear that I loved her.

They told me there wasn't a dry eye in the place. Every parent shared the emotion that stirred deep within me. And why not? The two most important commitments, indeed, the deepest loves of my life, had merged together in that moment: my love for my family and my commitment to the Christian faith. Fortunately, my daughter understood the feeling, and rather than being utterly embarrassed, she received it as a gift.

The world does not need another cold, stoic, "unfeeling clod," to use Shakespeare's phrase. But it is dying for men of genuine passion that grows out of the deepest convictions of their lives. I have been reclaiming the prayer that I first sang as a hymn at summer youth camp when I was my daughter's age:

> Teach me to love thee as thine angels love,
> one holy passion filling all my frame;

the kindling of the heaven-descended Dove,
my heart an altar, and thy love the flame.

Serving Others

Finally, I hope people will say that I loved this world and tried to change it. Contrary to the lines in the old gospel tune—"This world is not my home; I'm just a-passin' through"—this world is my home! This is the world God loved so much that God gave the Son, and we are called to love this world just as much as God did. As a follower of Jesus, I am called not only to pray that God's kingdom will come and that God's will be done on earth as it is in heaven, but also to live that way; to be a part of the coming of the rule of God in this world.

In February of 1968, Martin Luther King, Jr., preached a sermon at Ebenezer Church in Atlanta, in which he shared with his home congregation what he hoped people would say about him when he was gone. Portions of the tape of that sermon were played in the same church just four months later, at his funeral. Here are a few of Dr. King's words from *Testament of Hope*:

> If any of you are around when I have to meet my day . . . tell them not to mention that I have a Nobel Peace Prize, that isn't important. . . .
> I'd like somebody to mention that day that Martin Luther King, Jr., tried to give his life serving others . . . . I want you to say that day, that I tried to be right on the war question. I want you to be able to say that day, that I did try to feed the hungry . . . to clothe those who were naked . . . to visit those who were in prison. I want you to say that I tried to love and serve humanity. . . . I just want to leave a committed life behind. (p. 267)

Then he quoted the old gospel song:

> If I can help somebody as I pass along,
>   if I can cheer somebody with a word or song,
> if I can show somebody he's traveling wrong,
>   then my living will not be in vain.
> If I can do my duty as a Christian ought,
>   if I can bring salvation to a world once wrought,
> if I can spread the message as the master taught,
>   then my living will not be in vain.

What will it take for my life not to be in vain? What will they say about me when I'm gone? I hope they will say I loved this world and tried to be a part of its salvation.

Looking across my mid-life journey, I am now aware of a statement that has become a personal declaration of independence for me. I learned it from a pastor who was appointed to a church with a long history of conflict between the choir and the choir directors who would come and go. After working with the situation in every way he could imagine, he finally went to a rehearsal one evening, looked the choir members in the eye and said, "You know, folks, life is too short to be unhappy. If you can't find a way to be happy in this choir, perhaps you need to go somewhere else."

I have discovered genuine liberation in being able to say, "Life's too short"--not as an excuse for irresponsible behavior or as an easy escape from difficult challenges, but as a mile marker for the path I want my life to follow. "Life's too short," which is to say that I get only one chance at it, and when it's over I don't want to have used it in ways that do not satisfy my deepest sense of God's calling and my own sense of self-worth. Then my living will not have been in vain.

He Said/She Said

Jim: Do you think that answering the question, "What will they say about me when I'm dead and gone?" is a realistic way of looking at our lives?

Marsha: Yes, because it forces us to identify our priorities and helps us focus our energy on things that are meaningful to us.

Jim: Let's talk about consistency, the connection between the person we'd like to be and the way we really live. Were you surprised by any of the things I spelled out in this chapter?

Marsha: No, you've always been passionate about things you believed were important, and you have been very open about it. I feel that you have chosen your highest ideals, which is fine, but people also remember our faults and weaknesses.

We aren't perfect at this. Where does that fit in? You said one time that people die the way they live. If people are real and genuine about their best ideals, that's what others will remember, even recognizing all our human faults and failures.

If people are trying to fake it or pretend not to have any faults, others will see through it right away. The point is to be as honest and open as possible with one another.

Jim: Do you think that most folks are so busy managing the details of life that it is almost impossible for them to spend much time thinking about the kind of things I've described here?

Marsha: Absolutely! Days are filled with work, shopping, car pools, children, bill-paying, grass-cutting, and so forth. Most of us don't get much time to do this kind of thinking except on vacation. But that doesn't mean that it's not the right question to ask, and that once we start to ask it, there is the possibility that it could affect the way we live.

Action Plans for Him and Her

Him: What do you hope people will say about you after you're gone? How do you hope your children and grandchildren will remember you? Make your own list. In a sense, write your own eulogy. Make the list as specific as possible, defining clearly the commitments, values, and attitudes by which you hope your life will be measured.

Him: Share your list with your wife or a friend. Ask this person to help you evaluate how closely your statements would match what people would actually say about you if you died today. Be ruthlessly honest in evaluating the gaps between how you would like to be remembered and how you live right now.

Him: Compare your list to the attitudes and values that Jesus describes in the Beatitudes (Matt. 5). How closely are your values linked to Jesus' vision of life in the kingdom of God?

Her: Make your own list of the ways you hope you will be remembered. Compare your list to your husband's list, looking for the ways you share most in common and the ways you are most different. Talk together about how these similarities and differences affect your life together.

Him/Her: If you are parents, take a careful look at your relationship with your children. Measure the actual time each of you spend with them each week. List the things you do when you are together. Consider the emotional stress or exhaustion you may feel when you are with them at the end of the day. Then take a serious look at how you spend your money. As you consider the following questions, determine what changes you need to make in order for your relationship with your children to reflect the best ideals of your life:

- How do the ways you spend your money influence your children's understanding of what you value in life?
- What kind of attitudes are they learning from you?
- How is their vision of the world and other people being shaped by what they see in you?

Him/Her: From a practical standpoint, this is a good time to write or update your wills, to make sure your family's needs will be met if an unexpected tragedy should occur.

CHAPTER 12

Why Windshields Are Larger Than Rearview Mirrors

(Philippians 3:13b-14)

But this one thing I do: forgetting what lies behind and straining forward to what lies ahead, I press on toward the goal for the prize of the heavenly call of God in Christ Jesus.

I owe the title of this chapter to a friend named Dean Martin, who, until his death five years ago, was a nationally known pastor and chaplain for the Fighting Gators football team of the University of Florida. Dean had a knack for wrapping up big ideas in a simple phrase. That's what he did with this one. He said he learned it from a friend who was suddenly fired from his job. When Dean expressed his concern, his friend told him, "I'm looking ahead. I learned a long time ago that there is more glass in the windshield than there is in the rearview mirror."

It's true, of course. Windshields are significantly larger than rearview mirrors. The reason is obvious: When driving down the highway, it's more important to see where you are going than where you've been.

I learned that lesson as a college senior when I was student teaching at a high school in Kentucky. I was trying very hard to make a big impression on high school seniors who were only a few years younger than I. One day I was driving down the street in front of the school when I saw some of my students on the sidewalk. As I waved and smiled at them, I watched them in the mirror—right up to the moment when I plowed into the rear end of the car that had stopped at the red light in front of me! It made a big impression, but not the one I had intended!

That's not to say that rearview mirrors aren't important. We can't get along without them. How else would we know that the car with the flashing blue lights on top is coming after us? We need to know where we have been, and a part of the mid-life excursion leads us through the scrapbook of our past—the people and events that have made us the people we now are. But windshields are larger than rearview mirrors because it's even more important to see what lies ahead.

On the Move

There is solid biblical authority for the windshield image. The God of the Hebrew people was always on the move. God called Abraham and Sarah to leave their past behind and travel to a land they did not know. When God liberated the people of Israel from bondage in Egypt, they were called to follow the cloud and pillar across the wilderness toward a Promised Land. And who could forget Lot's unfortunate wife, who looked back and turned into a pillar of salt?

The Gospels are basically a travelogue with Jesus. He calls Peter, James, and John to leave their fishing nets and follow him on the road of discipleship. He calls Matthew to leave the tax collector's table and follow him on a way that leads to the cross. And at the empty tomb, the angel tells the women, "He has been raised; he is not here. . . . He is going ahead of you to Galilee; there you will see him" (Mark 16:6b-7).

We need rearview mirrors; we dare not forget those things that have shaped and nurtured our lives. But the Risen Christ is always out ahead of us, leading, calling, luring us to new life and new ways of thinking, living, and being.

You can feel the propelling thrust of that resurrection faith in the words of Paul. In the first letter to Corinth, he compares himself to an Olympic runner going for the prize (9:24-27). In the second letter, he paints a picture of the Roman legions returning victorious from battle, led along in a triumphant procession with fresh flowers strewn in their path (2:14-17). He sends this autobiographical witness to the Philippians: "Not that I have already obtained this or have already reached the goal; but I press on to make it my own . . . . But this one thing I do: forgetting what lies behind and straining forward to what lies ahead, I press on toward the goal for the prize of the heavenly call of God in Christ Jesus" (3:12-14).

People who follow Christ are always headed for a distant goal, always being led in a triumphal procession, always reaching out for what lies ahead. That's why windshields are larger than rearview mirrors.

Reaching Out for What Lies Ahead

For several reasons, I have conscientiously resisted using the word *crisis* to describe the mid-life experience. For one thing, the word carries a feeling of panic that results from an immediate, life-or-death situation, like rushing someone having a heart attack to the emergency room. Another reason is that it implies something that happens quickly and then is completed. Since neither of those factors is consistent with what most men experience at mid-life, I determined not to use the word. But then I remembered hearing that the Chinese symbol for *crisis* combines the symbols for *danger* and *opportunity*. If that is close to linguistic accuracy, it describes perfectly the realities that confront us.

Mid-life crisis is loaded with potential danger, growing largely out of a fear of loss brought on by the aging process—loss of youthful physical stamina, loss of sexual prowess, loss of ever-expanding career opportunities, loss of children as they leave home, and even loss of hair! Every study of men at mid-life contains some element of fear or danger. But mid-life also can be a time of opportunity. It can provide the opportunity to redefine our goals, to set new priorities, and to reach out with new faith and commitment for what lies ahead. Clinical psychologist Mark Gerzon points us in this direction by reframing the process as a "mid-life quest," which he describes as "the opening shot on a journey rather than the end of the line."

Savoring the Past

I had no way of knowing that mid-way through the work on this book I would face one of the major transitions of my life, a transition that fits all the definitions of the word *crisis*. I had watched my daughters graduate from high school and go off to college. My wife and I had made the initial transition to the empty nest more smoothly than we had imagined. Her career could hardly have been more satisfying. She was the second-grade teacher every parent hoped their child would have. She worked with an excellent faculty and was enjoying the challenge of leading the movement toward a year-round school calendar.

My work was a delight. After thirteen years, I had established deep relationships in the church and community. Because I knew that I needed new challenges to keep my ministry fresh, I was intentionally moving in new directions, fully expecting to continue to enjoy the results of the efforts that had gone into building one of the leading congregations in the area. My future felt exciting and secure.

Then it happened. On my forty-fifth birthday, I was asked to serve a church in another city.

I had shared similar emotions with so many men across the years. The phone call comes, and the voice on the other end of the line may say, "We're opening a new office in Baltimore and we need you there by the end of the month." Or, "The corporation is being reorganized because of the recent buy-out. The only opening we have for you is in Chicago." Or, worst of all, "You've done a fine job, but we don't have a place for you any longer. We will do everything we can to help you find a new position."

Our call came, and because we could feel the call of God within it, we said, "Yes," although describing it that simply does not begin to plumb the depths of personal and congregational pain involved.

Six months later, and on the way down that new road, I took a personal soul-retreat and sorted through some of the directional signs that have helped us along the way. The first marker instructed me to savor the past and feel the pain. There is no way to deny, avoid, or take a shortcut around the heartache that comes with change. We are never ready to take hold of what lies ahead until we feel the full weight of the loss of our past.

Paul acknowledges this in the Philippian letter when he lists everything he thought was important: circumcised on the eighth day, member of the people of Israel, of the tribe of Benjamin, a Pharisee, a persecutor of the church, blameless from the standpoint of the law (3:4-6). By describing the value these things held for him in the past, he measures the greater value of knowing Christ in the present and future.

We were fortunate to be part of an emotionally healthy congregation in which people were free to express their feelings: to laugh, to cry, to celebrate all that we had shared together. One of the most beautiful gifts came as an unexpected surprise the morning I shared the word of our impending move with the congregation. When I stood to announce the closing hymn, I was interrupted by a leading businessman. People who worked with him knew him as an exacting professional who kept his personal emotions well under control. But in a moment of spontaneous feeling, he rose and came down the aisle to stand facing the congregation.

Apologizing if he offended anyone, he said that he could not let the moment pass without saying how grateful he was for our years together and how much we would be missed. But he wanted me to know that I would go with the blessing and prayers of the congregation. Then he said, "I love you, Jim," and he wrapped his huge arms around me. To our surprise, the entire congregation stood with applause and tears as we hugged each other in the sacrament of Christian friendship. It was the beginning of a flow of genuine feeling, in which the healing process could begin.

A few days later I noticed the words that are etched on the mirror on the right side of my car: "Objects in mirror are closer than they appear." They are, you know; the past is always closer than it appears. The movement toward the future always involves the acceptance of our past.

But you can't spend your life looking in the rearview mirror, as I had learned that day I rear-ended the car ahead of me. That's why windshields are larger than rearview mirrors. That's why Paul was always looking ahead, always running toward another goal, always calling us to follow the living Christ, who always leads us in a great procession of faith.

Facing the Future

So after savoring the past and feeling the pain of loss, we began to reach out for what lies ahead. In contrast to being the organizing pastor of a new congregation, I would become the 29th pastor of a 91-year-old church! Rather than relating to a community where the majority of the homes had been constructed in the past ten years and most of the people had moved from somewhere else, I would live in one of the most historic neighborhoods in the state, with families that had been there for three or four generations. That's about enough change for anyone!

It was, in fact, the radical nature of the change that began to excite me. It was like discovering a whole new world, with new ways of thinking, new (to us) traditions, new tasks, and new responsibilities. At the same time, in the fellowship of the new community, we found elements of Christian friendship and fellowship similar to those we had left behind. With no attempt to deny the continuing pain of separation, we are beginning to discover the joy and challenge of what lies ahead. There continues to be a deep sense of God's Spirit, calling us to an unexpected and unpredictable future.

When E. Stanley Jones was eighty-three years old, he wrote his spiritual autobiography. He titled it *A Song of Ascents*, the title given some psalms in the Old Testament because they were sung by people on their way to worship in the Temple. In his introduction, Jones wrote:

I shall sing my song of the pilgrimage I am making from what I was to what God is making of me. . . . The best that I can say about myself is that I'm a Christian-in-the-making. Not yet "made" but only in the making at eighty-three. . . . So I face the future with confidence, even joy. . . . I am persuaded that the so-called end is just a beginning. . . . Jesus is Lord—Lord of the past, Lord of the present, Lord of the future. Jesus is Lord of everything. . . . A conclusion which is a beginning. (pp. 366-67, 372)

Conclusions are never easy. Beginnings are not all that great, either. And transitional periods in our lives can be the pits. The ability to face the future with confidence, even joy, is dependent not upon the circumstances, but upon the faith we bring to them. That faith is rooted in the confident assurance that we follow a living Lord who goes before us into an unknown future and will meet us there with new grace, new possibilities, and new strength.

One of the gifts received by Walt Whitman on his seventieth birthday was a card from Mark Twain with these words: "Yes, you have indeed seen much—but tarry for a while, for the greatest is yet to come."

That's visionary faith, and that's why windshields are larger than rearview mirrors.

He Said/She Said

Jim: Well, what can we say about our mutual mid-life crisis in saying good-bye to the familiar and looking ahead to the future?

Marsha: You're right: It's painful and it's tough. There is no way around that. The toughest part for me has been the separation from friendships. As I shared before, it takes time for me to develop deep friendships, and that means that it's really hard to leave them and start all over. Second only to separation from friends was the difficulty in finding and starting a new job. I left a situation where I was known, trusted, and respected, and where I knew how things worked. Now I'm starting all over again in a new place, with new people, in a different setting. That's been tough. I wouldn't be honest if I didn't say that there have been days when I've resented having to make the change.

Jim: I know that feeling, too, and it's not a negative reflection on the new situation. I'm fascinated that I can feel both pain about where we left and excitement about where we are. But I also know that it is usually easier for the one who moves into a new job situation than for the family that has to go along.

Marsha: Although I shared in the decision, there's also a sense in which the girls and I had no choice; we simply had to go along. I know we aren't unique in that, but I think it's important to honestly acknowledge those feelings.

Jim: What has been most helpful in all of this?

Marsha: As you said, we left a very healthy group of people who could share their real feelings together. There were lots of tears along with lots of laughter. It made the separation go better. We were able to leave without feeling that we had left a lot of "unfinished business" behind. I can also look ahead and see people whom I know will become great friends and new things that I know will happen. Beneath it all is a deep awareness that this is what the Lord called us to do. That makes a world of difference. We know that God is in this and that everything will be all right.

Action Plans for Him and Her

Him: Read Philippians 3:1-16 in several different translations. Then paraphrase the passage in your own words, describing your own experience of the past, the present, and the future. If you have kept a journal, read back through it as you reflect on the passage.

Him/Her: Make a list of the primary concerns or personal goals for the second half of your journey. Share those with your spouse or friend. Pray about them together and make a covenant for your future.

Him/Her: Consider gathering a group of men or couples who can help one another cope with the challenges of the "mid-life quest" by sharing and discussing their own experiences. The group may find it helpful to read and discuss this book or another one like it.

CHAPTER 13

Keep Your Eyes on the Road

Hebrews 12:3*b*, 12-13 GNB

Do not let yourselves become discouraged and give up. . . . Lift up your tired hands, then, and strengthen your trembling knees! Keep walking on straight paths, so that the lame foot may not be disabled, but instead be healed.

So, here I am: a forty-five-year-old male, husband and father, approaching his silver wedding anniversary, who just completed the twentieth year in his career, made a major move to a job in a new city, and was recently hospitalized with heart trouble. I have two kids in college, a mortgage, graying hair, and a fairly healthy libido. You can't be much more "mid-life" than that! I think I've been through the crisis stage of my mid-life detour, and with the resources of a great family, a healthy faith, and honest friends, I'm on the road toward a different and better second half.

As soon as I write that description, however, I remember the retired friend who said, "Jim, take it from me. It's true at forty-five, it's true at fifty-five, and it's still true at sixty-five: You never escape the crisis that comes with change."

In the classic words of John Cardinal Newman, "Dangers and hopes appear in new relations; and old principles reappear under new forms. It changes with them in order to remain the same. In a higher world it is otherwise, but here below to live is to change, and to be perfect is to have changed often."

The ultimate issue for mid-life travelers is the same for people of both sexes and of almost any age. It is the issue of change and how we respond to it. With all the distractions within and around us, can we still keep our eyes on the road?

The folks who received the New Testament letter to the Hebrews were at a critical point of transition. They were second-generation Christians. The first-generation Christians had been convinced that Jesus was coming back soon—any day, next week at the latest. But the days turned into weeks and the weeks into years. Jesus didn't return as they expected. The children grew up and started families of their own.

The apostles and all those folks who were there on Pentecost started to die off. Now these second-generation Christians had to find a new identity. They had to discover what it would mean to live the faith in their own day and time. So the writer of this letter encourages them: "Do not let yourselves become discouraged and give up. . . . Lift up your tired hands, then, and strengthen your trembling knees!" (Heb. 12:3b, 12 GNB).

The journey toward maturity, the road that leads toward wholeness, requires us to continually change our plans, alter our course, redirect our path. The critical factor is not the detours along the way but the clarity with which we keep our eyes on the destination.

Getting Rid of Excess Baggage

The writer of this letter to the Hebrews offers some practical advice to keep us on course. First, we are challenged to get rid of excess baggage—the old habits, old attitudes, old sins that get tangled around our feet and keep us from moving forward—so that we may "run with determination the race that lies before us" (Heb. 12:1c GNB).

A major part of our movement toward maturity is learning what to give away. Every now and then the Spirit says to us, "It's time to grow up and get rid of old childish attitudes, fears, prejudices, and hurts, and move toward the maturity God intends for you. Get rid of anything that gets tangled around your feet, and get going on the trek of life and faith."

Paul talks about the same thing in his first letter to Corinth: "When I was a child, I spoke like a child, I thought like a child, I reasoned liked a child; when I became an adult, I put an end to childish ways" (13:11).

In *Putting Away Childish Things,* David Seamands describes the "inner child of our past," the childhood experiences that continue to influence our behavior. Often when we confront some crisis in life, we suddenly discover that we are being driven, motivated, or controlled by some petty childish attitude caused by some pain in our early life. Seamands would say that when your response to a specific situation is out of proportion to the event, you can suspect that the little child within is in control. Growing out of his years of practical pastoral counseling experience, Seamands describes the way God's grace can help us confront, name, acknowledge, forgive, and be set free from the little child of our past.

I've seen that child in my own life and in the lives of countless people with whom I have struggled. Dealing with it is like the writer of the letter to the Hebrews telling us to get rid of those things that keep us from the healthy maturity God intends. One of the best known examples of this truth is found in Adult Children of Alcoholics (ACOA), which helps adults deal with the way their behaviors have been influenced by their parents' addictive personalities. I have seen miraculous changes in men and women who honestly face their past, name it, confront it, and forgive it, to find healing in the present and hope for the future. It may not be easy. In fact, it may be downright painful. But it is necessary for our journey toward maturity.

Fixing Your Eyes on Jesus

The writer of the letter to the Hebrews also advises us to "keep our eyes fixed on Jesus, on whom our faith depends from beginning to end" (12:2 GNB). This verse in the Revised Standard Version describes Jesus as "the pioneer and perfecter of our faith." Today we might use the term "role model" to describe Jesus as the one and only healthy and mature person in whose likeness we hope to grow.

What would maturity be like if you really attained it? What would it be like for you to become a whole, free person? What will you be like if you actually become the person you are now in the process of becoming? What do you think you are going to be when you grow up?

We know the importance of role models as the pattern for the kind of person we want to be. The most frightening thing about the movie *Wall Street* is that it is so real. It is the story of a young stock broker, played by Charlie Sheen, who sets out to become a success. He takes as his mentor a ruthless mover and shaker on the Street, played by Michael Douglas, who announces the practical theology of the 1980s in America: "Greed is good."

We watch as the younger man begins to dress, act, talk, and think like his mentor, until, just in the nick of time, something snaps. He suddenly realizes that the person he is becoming is not the person he most deeply wants to be. He breaks the cycle and goes a different way.

If you fully became the person you are now becoming, who would you be like? The writer of this letter said, "Let us keep our eyes fixed on Jesus." He is the one-and-only, all-time, genuine, original model of human wholeness and maturity. Keep your eyes fixed on him. Read his story in the Gospels. Listen to his words. Watch his actions. Feel his compassion. See how he relates to others. Look at his influence on human history. Open your mind, your life, your soul, to the invading presence of his Spirit. Then you'll begin to discover the whole person that God intends for you to be.

Phillips Brooks was one of the most influential religious leaders of the nineteenth century in America. Toward the end of his life, he received a letter from a young man who asked if he would tell him the secret of his life. Note the present-tense verbs in Brooks' answer:

> I have no secrets. The last years have had a peace and fullness which there did not used to be. I'm sure it is a deeper knowledge and truer love of Christ. I cannot tell you how personal this grows to me. He is here. He knows me and I know him. It is not a figure of speech. It is the most real thing in the world. And every day makes it more real. And one wonders with delight what it will grow to as the years go on.

As I prepared to send my older daughter off to the university for the first time, I found myself feeling the need to say something—something like that humorous scene in *Hamlet* when Polonius gives his interminable farewell advice to Laertes. Fortunately, my daughter told me that there was nothing I needed to say that she hadn't heard already. But I did find a book that I tucked away in her boxes and sent with her. And I did it again two years later when my younger daughter made the same journey. The book, *Letters to Marc About Jesus,* is a collection of personal letters written by Henri Nouwen to his nineteen-year-old nephew in Holland.

In the opening chapter, Nouwen describes the way his studies and work have taken him around the world, working with Protestants and Catholics, Christians and humanists, radical revolutionaries and traditional patriots, rich and poor, sick and healthy. Then he says, "In every phase of my search I've discovered that Jesus Christ stands at the center of my seeking. If you were to ask me point-blank, 'What does it mean for you to live spiritually?' I would have to reply, 'Living with Jesus at the center.'"

Nouwen confesses, as all of us must, that he continues to have doubts, questions, problems, and difficulties that demand attention. He admits that there have been times when immediate problems have pushed his awareness of Jesus into the background. But then he goes on:

> Despite this, when I look back over the last thirty years of my life, I can say that, for me, the person of Jesus has come to be more and more important. Increasingly, what matters is getting to know Jesus and living in solidarity with him. . . . It has become clearer to me than ever that my personal relationship with Jesus is the heart of my existence. (p. 7)

He concludes with these exciting words, which express my deepest prayer and highest hope for both my daughters:

> Living with Jesus is a great adventure. It's the adventure of love. When you admit Jesus to your heart nothing is predictable, but everything becomes possible. I pray that you will venture on a life with Jesus. He asks everything of you, but gives you more in return. With all my heart I wish you much hope, much courage, and abounding confidence. (pp. 84-85)

Not only is that a good place to begin the journey as a college freshman, but it is also a great way to begin the second half of the journey.

He Said/She Said

Jim: How are we different in our response to change?

Marsha: Like most women, I'm the one who has had to make major changes because of movement in your career. I sometimes wonder how you would cope if it were the other way around. I know that happens more often now, with changes in women's careers, but it's still the exception. This means that the difference in the way we deal with change has something to do with the fact that many times we have little control over the change. When you get down to it, the real point here is that we can make the choice to focus on Jesus as the central factor in our life. At that point, we're on common ground.

Jim: How have we "put away" childish things across the years?

Marsha: The first thing that comes to mind is in relation to the girls. As we have grown up with them, there have been times when I discovered that I could still love them, even if they disagreed with some of my personal convictions or refused to follow what I wanted for them. I learned to be more tolerant, more accepting.

Jim: Does that go for me as well? How have you had to learn to be more tolerant, more accepting of the differences between us?

Marsha: When we were first married, I thought we had to agree on everything, particularly spiritual things. Now I realize that we can have different ideas, different understandings of scripture, and different ways of expressing our faith, without feeling that either of us is less Christian than the other. We can enjoy different things and respond to things differently, without it being a threat to the health of our relationship. God accepts us and loves us the way we are. We've tried to love our kids this way, even when they don't agree with us. We've learned to love each other this way, too.

Jim: With all these differences, what holds us together?

Marsha: Just what you said: The central piece that holds us together is that we sincerely want Christ to be at the center of our lives. Everything else should revolve around that commitment. With that, life can be a great adventure.

Action Plans for Him and Her

These action plans will help you take a personal inventory of your life and faith.

Him: If you actually became the person you are now becoming, what would you be like? Write down in your journal the central beliefs, values, and hopes of your life and faith, as well as the characteristics of your personality. Share these with your spouse or friend.

Him: What are some of the childish things you need to lay aside to move toward maturity? Choose one of these and identify steps you can take this week to "lay it aside."

Him: What does it mean for you to live with Jesus at the center of your life? Choose one of the four Gospels and begin reading a chapter each day. Focus on how Jesus speaks, acts, and relates to others. As you open yourself to the presence of his Spirit, you will begin to discover the person God intends you to be.

Her: Make a list of the new discoveries you have made about the man in your life as you have read this book. How do these discoveries change the way you will relate to him in the future?

Him/Her: Based on what you have read and discussed together, make your own "travel plans" for the future of your relationship. List the changes you want to make and the goals you want to establish, and how you will be accountable for their fulfillment. Confirm this covenant spiritually by sharing together in the Sacrament of Holy Communion the next time it is available in your church.

Resources for the Journey

Edward Klein and Don Erickson, ed. *About Men: Reflections on the Male Experience.* New York: Poseidon Press, 1987.

Balswick, Jack. *Men at the Crossroads.* Downers Grove, Ill.: InterVarsity Press, 1992.

Bly, Robert. *Iron John.* Reading, Mass.: Addison Wesley, 1990.

Dillard, Annie. *An American Childhood.* New York: Harper & Row, 1987.

Gerzon, Mark. *Coming Into Our Own: Understanding Adult Metamorphosis.* New York: Delacorte, 1992.

Goldstein, Ross E. *Fortysomething.* Los Angeles: Jeremy P. Tarcher, 1990.

Hammarskjold, Dag. *Markings.* New York: Alfred A. Knopf, 1966.

Hawkins, David, and Ross Tunnell. *Reclaiming Manhood.* Wheaton, Ill.: Victor Books, 1992.

Jones, E. Stanley. *A Song of Ascents.* Nashville: Abingdon Press, 1968.

Joy, Donald. *Unfinished Business.* Wheaton, Ill.: Victor Books, 1989.

Keen, Sam. *Fire In the Belly*. New York: Bantam Books, 1991.

Marty, Martin. *Friendship*. Allen, Tex.: Argus Communications, 1980.

Mayer, Nancy. *The Male Mid-Life Crisis*. New York: Signet, 1978.

Nelson, James B. *The Intimate Connection: Male Sexuality, Masculine Spirituality*. Philadelphia: Westminster Press, 1988.

Nouwen, Henri. *Letters to Marc About Jesus*. San Francisco: Harper & Row, 1988.

Shedd, Charlie W. *Remember, I Love You: Martha's Story*. New York: HarperCollins, 1980. (See other Shedd books, including, *Talk to Me; How to Stay in Love; Bible Study Together: Making Marriage Last;* and *Praying Together: Making Marriage Last*.)

Stoop, David. *Making Peace with Your Father*. Wheaton, Ill.: Tyndale, 1992.